Grandma's Antique Recipes:

The legacy of a Lancashire Lass

By Patricia Matthews

Recipes, remedies and tips from a bygone age

Who was Grandma Sarah?

Sarah Tindsley was born in Salford Lancashire on the 8th of August 1893 in the reign of Queen Victoria. She was one of seven children and the only daughter of Elizabeth and Edwin Tindsley. In the 1901 Census of England and Wales Sarah and her family moved to Bolton and were living at number 21 Apple Street in the district of Bolton le Moors Emmanuel, a district of Bolton Lancashire. Later in 1911, the census shows that the family had moved to a different address in Bolton to number 65, Thynne Street Bolton, nearer to the town centre, this street still exists today I travel along it regularly on my way to the town centre. Here in Bolton she met and married Grandpa Norman, and according to family information, Grandma Sarah and Grandpa Norman worked and met whilst working the same cotton mill in Bolton.

Bolton at that time, was like most other Lancashire towns and the main employment was in the cotton mills a thriving industry at the time, creating much employment for the people of Bolton and the skyline was awash with the tall brick chimneys and red brick mills. On the 30th of December 1915, at the Kings Hall Wesleyan Methodist Chapel Bradshawgate Bolton, Sarah Tindsley (Spinster) and Norman Matthews (Bachelor) tied the knot and began their married life together.

**Grandma Sarah,
the Lancashire lass
and her legacy**

First published in the United Kingdom 2013.

A catalogue record of this book is available from the British Library.

ISBN 978-1-907463-82-2

SHN Publishing
www.shnpublishing.com

Contents

Preface

Dear cooking enthusiasts everywhere. I would like to introduce you all to this hand-written gem of a book written by Grandma Sarah, containing 160 authentic and used recipes for cakes, cures, medicines, furniture polishes, and handy hints from long ago. This was left to me by her, along with her wedding ring, which I had re-modelled to use as my own on my wedding day.

Sarah Tindsley was born in Salford on the 8th August 1893. She was one of seven children. She moved to Bolton and in 1915 she married Norman Matthews, and together they had one son. Grandma Sarah was a God-fearing Christian with strong morals and strong beliefs, and she was also a comic and an excellent mimic. She was an exceptional cook and when we visited her we would always look forward to her baking, accompanied by copious mugs of tea and chats.

In the contents of this nostalgic little recipe book there are recipes for cakes, cures, medicines, furniture polishes, wood stains and handy hints from bygone days; they were all hand-written and handed down for other young wives in the family to use. I find it fascinating to think that they made their own cures, medicines, furniture polishes, and wood stain, but we have to remember that in the early 1900's when this book was in use, this would be before the National Health was established, and if a doctor was called upon to visit the sick then he would expect to be paid by the family.

I also would imagine that money would be very tight so they relied on tried and tested cures handed down to them by the family and relatives, also, some of the ingredients used in those days are unavailable now, they have of course been substituted by safer and more modern medicines, but much to my amusement and dismay they were for a long time standard use within the home for illness and complaints.

As I thumbed through the fascinating contents of this gem of a book, it gave me an insight into aspects of Grandma Sarah's everyday life, and the things that seemed important to her such as family, church, neighbours, community and pride – these were everything to them.

I hope you find this book and its contents a fascinating read, and

Dedication

Kathleen Joan Runciman (nee Matthews).
Forever in our thoughts.

1946 – 2013.

Acknowledgement:

First and fourmost to Grandma Sarah for the little gem of a cook
book and all the happy memories.

To SHN Publishing, especially to Stephen, for his support,
advice, and his belief in this project.
Thank You.

The Bolton History museum.

To my family for their help, encouragement and support.

Equipment

To all you cooking enthusiasts and friends of baking like me, I just thought I'd mention that in cooking, it doesn't have to cost a fortune, and you don't have to buy expensive equipment especially if you're on a budget. If you have the basic essentials then you can make any of the recipes in this book. Grandma Sarah and ladies of her era didn't have food mixers, blenders, bread machines and the like but they still managed to cook up some very tasty wholesome meals.

All you need is enthusiasm and practice, elbow grease, (effort) and a love of food. In my view you only need the minimum equipment to cook, of course all the recipes in the book can be made in food processors and the modern equipment we have today and that is fine. I have noticed however, some of the cakes and puddings etc when cooked, are a little different in texture, for instance the sponges are not as light as the ones we make today, but never the less are just as tasty.

As I mentioned previously, this is due to the choice of flours, ingredients and cookers that were used in the homes and kitchens of housewives and mothers of Grandma Sarah's time, and it was only when the first thermostatically controlled gas and electric cookers were available and affordable, I suppose cooking for the family became a lot easier as they no longer had to build up the fire in the hearth to heat the cast iron ovens, to bake the bread and pies and such, although this method of cooking by solid fuel was used in working class family homes for a long time, I should guess it was the 1950's before gas and electric cookers became the norm in households around the North West of England.

So, if the recipes turn out a little different, but just as tasty, remember, when you eat them you'll be sharing and tasting a little bit of history from bygone times from the era of Grandma Sarah and the ladies of her time.

- Essential Equipment
- Large Bowl
- Wooden Spoon
- Rolling Pin
- Scales
- Whisk
- Skillet
- Pallet knife
- Good Quality Baking tray
- Good quality cake tin

Old Money, Imperial Measures
& School Life in Yesteryear

Maths

Do the young people of today know how simple their maths lessons are compared to Grandma Sarah's and my own? I'm going to take you on a journey back in time when the schools of yesterday were austere, strict, and unwelcoming. Discipline was tough and unforgiving and in some cases schools were terrifying places for some kids, especially the maths lessons.

Times tables were recited religiously every morning before the register was taken and then we all went into the school hall for assembly.

At school children were taught the imperial units of measure and money, today we use metrication were every measurement is based on ten.

With Imperial there was no common connection to the units so each had to be learned and memorised off by heart which I can tell you was no easy task.

As far as I know this system of teaching maths had been used in schools since about 1870's onwards until decimalisation came in the 1970's.

In Cookery, the utensils would be very different from today's electronic equipment. Scales with copper pans and round cast iron weight's would have been used to measure out the ingredients; they would consist of a 2lb, 1lb, 8oz, 1oz, ½ oz and ¼ oz weight. Jugs with indented markings on the side were used for liquids, and sometimes in the face of economy, a milk bottle was used instead of a rolling pin. Below are some pictures of the sort of equipment that would have been used in the kitchen of Grandma Sarah's early married life. This equipment is still available to buy today from the internet, under the title of vintage and below are some examples to give you some idea.

IMPERIAL MEASURES

Units of length

1 inch (in or ")
= 25.4mm

12 inches (ins)
= 1 foot = 305 mm

3 feet (ft)
= 1 yard = 0.91mm

1760 yards (yrds)
= 1 mile (m) = 1.61 km

144 square ins (sq in)
= 1 sq foot

9 square feet (sq ft)
= 1 square yard

4840 sq.yards (sq yrds)
= 1 acre about the size of a football pitch.

5 ½ yards
= 1 rod pole or perch??

22 yards
= 1 chain (incidentally, this is the length of a cricket pitch)

10 chains
= 1 furlong
8 furlongs
= 1 mile.
Then 220 yards in 1 furlong and 1,760 yards in a mile.

Units of weight

16 drams (dr)
= 1 ounce = tablespoon of sugar = 28 grams

16 ounces (oz)
= 1lb (pound) = 0.45 kg a bag of sugar. Written this way to avoid confusion with the £1

14 lbs
= 1 st (stone) used in body weight = 6.35 kg

2 stone
= 1 quarter = 12.7 kg

4 quarters
= 1 hundred weight = 112 lbs a bag of cement = 50.8 kg

8 stones
= 1 cwt (hundredweight)

20 cwt
= 1 ton Then there was 112lbs in 1cwt and 2,240lbs in 1 ton.

Capacity as it was known.

5 fluid ounces = 1 gill = 142ml

4 gills = 1 pint

1 pint = 20 fluid ounces = an English beer = 568 ml

2 pints (pts) = 1 quart a German beer = 1.1 L

4 quarts (qrt) = 1 gallon = a large tin of paint = 4.546 L

2 gallons (galls) = 1 peck   9.1 L

4 pecks = 1 bushel.

And then there was the money to get to grips with:

I can remember the wear and tear on the pockets of trousers due to the sheer weight of the coins carried around day by day. Housewives of the day were always either mending or replacing pockets in jackets and trousers.

2 farthings
= 1 halfpenny pronounced 'hapepenny'= 0.208p

4 farthings
= 1 penny (d) abbreviation for the Latin denarius or dinar = 0.417p

3 pennies
= 1 threepenny bit this was a brass coin with 12 sides and there was an older silver one which was small and round. They used them to put in Birthday cakes and Wedding cakes and if you happen to get one in your piece of cake (Gulp) it was considered lucky. = 1.25p

6 pennies
= 1 sixpenny piece this was the first coin in nickel = 2.5p

12 pennies
= 1 shilling it was known as a bob as in 'bob a job' = 5p

2 shillings
= 1 florin = 10p

2s-6p; 2/6d
= 1 half a crown the biggest coin in regular use = 12.5p

10 shillings
= 1 ten 'bob' note, this was the first in paper money = 50p

20 shillings
= 1 pound note (quid) there were also £5 notes and £10 notes.

Just a Thought

As I browse through this little gem of a book, I realise that the choice of baking ingredients for the everyday recipes were limited compared to the vast choice of baking aids we have today. I suppose it relied on the availability of ingredients needed, the seasons, and the money in their pocket. The housewives of yesterday didn't seem to have the variety of flour or fats or flavours we have today.

Cookery is much more scientific nowadays, and we learn in school about which ingredients reacts with which, what type of flour is best for what kind of recipe and so on.

I noticed for instance that in the jams and preserves, no pectin or lemon juice is used, whether that was deliberate or not I can't say, I think the wives and mothers of the 1920's 30's and 40's used the fruit which was most plentiful and by trial and error chose the ones which gave the best results for the jams and preserves.

This particular way of making recipes and produce would nowadays be known as ARTISAN.

Artisan refers to a time when people took their time and made things by hand and in a traditional way.

The fruits used in the recipes in Grandma Sarah's book, contain a lot of acidity and flavour so, maybe that's the reason they were so popular, also people could pick the fruits for free as they grew wild all around, and we must remember also that ordinary folk of the day had large families and would not have had refrigerators to keep any food fresh.

The housewives of yesteryear used what was available to them from day to day but, whether cakes and breads or any recipes, were of the same quality and texture as we have today I don't know, but they made the best of what they could afford for their families.

Hints from Grandma Sarah

In the book Grandma Sarah wrote down some handy hints to help in her everyday running of the house chores, these were probably handed down from her mother, after all I should imagine she played a large part in helping out in their home when she was growing up, especially as she was the only girl amongst six brothers. Some of them you may have heard of and some of them you will be less familiar with, I think they are charming.

A tablespoon of Glycerine in the starch water makes ironing a pleasure.

If milk is just going to boil over place a Silver spoon in the pan and this will stop the milk from boiling over.

Mint sauce eaten with lamb, is improved by dissolving a teaspoon of sugar in two tablespoons of boiling water and pour over the mint and leave for 10 minutes before adding the vinegar.

A tablespoon of boiling water added to sponge mix makes lighter sponge cakes.

To help green vegetables keep their colour boil in the pan without the lid.

When pickling onions or red cabbage, crispness may be obtained if a pinch of Alum? is used.

Before whisking eggs, rinse the bowl with cold water and leave a drop or two in the bottom, the eggs will then come out clean and this will save waste.

The best way of making curdled custard smooth is to stand it in a pan of cold water and beat with an egg whisk until smooth.

To prevent skin forming on boiled milk, cover the pan with a plate or saucer, thus saving all the goodness.

When making oatmeal porridge or cooking rice, if the pot is greased with lard or butter first it is much easier to clean.

Save the green leaves of celery, dry them in the oven, then rub down into a powder and store them in a glass jar, they make good flavourings for soups and stews.

Here's a bit of advice for us all.

Where you go wrong.

You do not dry the fruit thoroughly which tends to make your cake heavy.

I think she meant: If you do not dry the washed fruit thoroughly before you add it to the cake mixture it will make the cake heavy and stodgy.

You do not have the oven hot enough, when browning the cake, the cake is left in too long and it becomes over cooked. Five minutes should be long enough.

Here, I think she was advising to preheat the oven at the correct regulo (temp) for five minutes.

The early recipes in the book would have most probably been cooked on an oven heated by the fire. These oven combinations were known as "Bungalow Ranges" these were the most common ones used by the working classes they were built into the chimney breasts of the houses and were fuelled by coal or coke. As time went on the gas cooker came on the scene, this was basic but it had a more controlled heat by the introduction of the thermostat and the regulo, the temperatures on the thermostat ranged from regulo 1 to regulo 10 giving a more controlled heat for better baking. There was also more upmarket ones these were known as the AGA cookers these cookers were first imported from Sweden to Britain in 1929 and they are still sought after, and still in use today. As we travel through the book we can get an idea of the progress made in the kitchen, by the ingredients available, the recipe methods and the appliances used.

These will help people who are without scales:

- 1 tablespoon of flour = 1oz
- 1 level tablespoon of castor sugar = ½ oz
- 1 rounded tablespoon of jam, honey treacle or syrup = 2ozs
- 2 heaped tablespoons of breadcrumbs = 1oz
- 1 egg weight approximately 3ozs
- 1 gill liquid or 7 tablespoons of water = ¼ pint

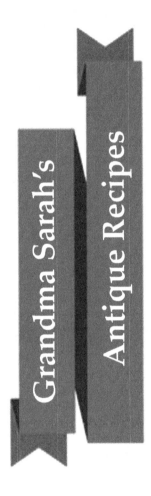

Grandma Sarah's Recipes

Patent Flour

In certain recipes in this nostalgic little cookery book, Patent Flour is used, and I wondered if this type of flour was what we know as Self-Raising flour? I don't know! I'll have to do some research. Below is Grandma Sarah's recipe for Patent Flour.

- 2 ½ lb flour
- 1 ½ oz of Cream of tartar
- ½ oz of Carbonate soda

Research shows that Patent Flour was a high-grade flour, selected from the purest streams in the flour mill and was free of impurities. It was mainly used in bread making for which it was most suitable but special varieties are needed for some confectionary purposes.

Patent Flour

Patent flour is classified in five categories depending on the amount of straight flour it contains.

Extra Short or fancy patent flours are made from soft wheats and are used for cakes.

Short Patent flour made from hard wheat is recommended for bread making, so is medium patent flour, and it is up to the baker to decide which flour serves his or her purpose best.

Apparently there are many type of flours:

- Straight flour
- Cake flour
- Pastry flour
- All-purpose flour

Patent Flour

High gluten flour. And many more, all of them have specific uses, but personally I'll just stick to the supermarket one I always use.

Grandma Sarah's
Jams and Preserves

Blackcurrant Jam

- 3lb Blackcurrants
- 1 Quart of water (2 pints)
- 4 ½ lbs of sugar

- Boil the fruit and water for 20mins add the sugar and boil for a further 15min.

- First of all, sterilise the jam jars and the lids by placing them into a large pan, cover with water and boil them for about 10 mins.

- Remove them with tongs and drain onto a tea towel and leave to cool. Repeat this for all the jars you use for the following recipes.

- Place two or three saucers into the freezer.
- Label when cold.

Blackcurrant Jam

- Wash the fruit, transfer the blackberries into a large pan, add 2 pints of water and boil gently for 20 mins, stirring from time to time.

- Add the sugar and boil rapidly for a further 15min until setting point is reached, keep stirring the pan to avoid sticking or burning.

- Test the setting point: take one of the plates from the freezer take the jam off the heat and spoon a little on to the plate and leave to cool. If the jam is set, spoon into warm jam jars, cover and seal, label when cold.

Apricot Jam

- 1lb apricots
- Steep (soak) in water for 24hrs
- 4lb sugar

Boil in the water they have been soaked in, and add the sugar.

In this recipe, there isn't much information, but I'm assuming that the method is the same as for the blackcurrant jam but making sure that the apricots are stoned and halved first.

Damson Jam

- 6lb Damsons
- 6lb sugar
- 1 gill (1pint) water

Once again, Grandma Sarah didn't bother with detailed methods in most recipes, this, I assume, is because she made them so often she didn't see the need but I would imagine that it's the same or similar method as the other two jam recipes but once again make sure that all the stones from the damsons have been removed before it is spooned into the jars.

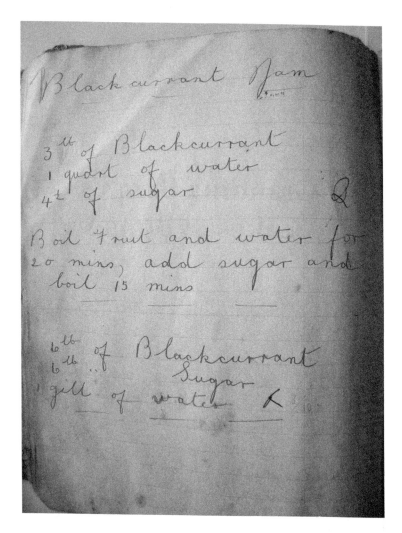

Grandma Sarah's original blackcurrant jam recipe in her original handwriting

Grandma Sarah's
Cakes & Buns

Cherry Buns

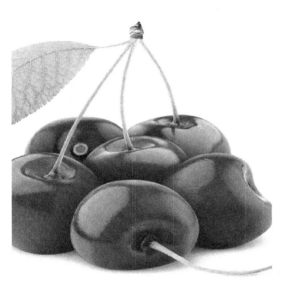

Grandma Sarah's CAKES and BUNS

- 6ozs/ 170g Self raising Flour
- 2ozs/60g Sugar
- 3oz/80g Butter/margarine
- 2 tablespoons Milk
- 2ozs/60g Glace cherries

Pre heat the oven 220⁰C/424⁰F/gas 7

- Cream the butter and sugar together until the mixture is light and creamy.

- Add the beaten egg.

- Cut the cherries into quarters and add to the flour.

Cherry Buns

Grandma Sarah's CAKES and BUNS

- Gently fold in the flour to the creamed mixture and mix thoroughly, add the milk gradually until the mixture is a soft dropping consistency.

- Grease a deep bun tray and fill with ¾ of the mixture.

- Bake for 15/20 minutes until well risen and golden brown.

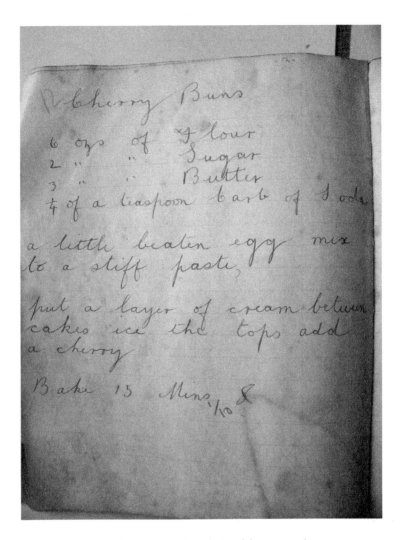

**Grandma Sarah's original buns recipe
in her original handwriting**

Cherry Cake

Grandma Sarah's CAKES and BUNS

- 8ozs/200g Flour
- ½ Teaspoon Baking Powder
- 4ozs/100g Butter
- 4ozs/100g sugar
- 4ozs Glace cherries
- 2 Eggs
- 1 Tablespoonful of milk

Preheat the oven to 150⁰C/ gas 4/5

- Line and grease a 6" cake tin.

- Cut up the cherries and toss in a little flour (this stops them sinking to the bottom of the cake) and set aside.

Cherry Cake

Grandma Sarah's — CAKES and BUNS

- Cream the fat and sugar until it's light and fluffy.
- Add the eggs one at a time with a little of the flour to stop them curdling and mix well.
- Fold in the remaining flour and cherries if the mixture feels too stiff, add a little of the milk.
- The mixture should drop easily off the spoon.
- Spoon the mixture into cake the tin.
- Bake in the oven for 55-mins to1hour.
- Leave in the tin for 10mins to cool.
- Turn out onto a wire rack and leave until completely cold before serving.

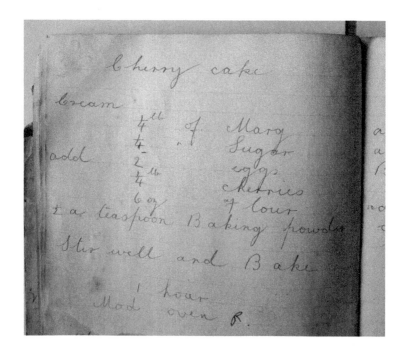

**Grandma Sarah's original cherry cake recipe
in her original handwriting**

Chocolate Cake

Grandma Sarah's CAKES and BUNS

- 8ozs/200g Self Raising Flour
- 4ozs/100g Butter
- 4ozs/100g Sugar
- 2 Eggs
- 3ozs/75g of Cocoa or Chocolate
- 2 Tablespoons of milk
- Lemon essence

Preheat oven to 150°C/gas 5

- Line and grease 8" sandwich tin or use two 7" tins.

- Dissolve the chocolate/cocoa in the milk and stir to a smooth cream and set aside.

Chocolate Cake

Grandma Sarah's CAKES and BUNS

- Cream the fat in the bowl with a wooden spoon until soft.

- Add the sugar and beat until the mixture is light in colour and fluffy.

- Add the lemon essence.

Chocolate Cake

Grandma Sarah's CAKES and BUNS

- Add the eggs one at a time with a little of the sieved flour then add the chocolate/cocoa and mix well.
- Fold in the remaining flour.
- Spoon the mixture into the tin.
- And level with a palette knife or table knife.
- Bake for 25-30 mins or until the sponge feels firm to the touch.
- Leave in the tin for 10 mins.
- When cold, cut in half, spread with chocolate butter, sandwich together and ice with chocolate icing, or butter cream.
- Decorate to your liking.

Chocolate icing
- 4ozs/100g of plain chocolate
- 6ozs/72g sieved icing sugar
- Small knob of butter

Chocolate Cake

Grandma Sarah's CAKES and BUNS

- 2-2 ½ tablespoons of warm water.
- Break the chocolate into small pieces and put it and the butter into a small pan with 1 ½ tablespoons of warm water.
- Stir over a gentle heat until it is a smooth creamy consistency.
- Cool the mixture until it's lukewarm.
- Add the icing sugar little by little, beating thoroughly, and keep adding a little warm water.
- Return to the heat and beat until the icing is at a coating consistency.
- Pour over the cake and decorate with sugar flowers.

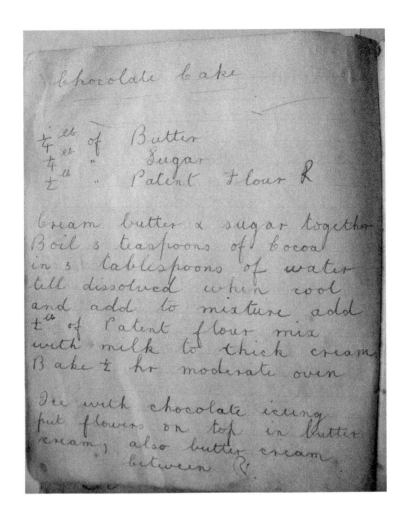

**Grandma Sarah's original chocolate cake recipe
in her original handwriting**

Christmas Cake

Grandma Sarah's

CAKES and BUNS

- 12oz Plain Flour
- 8oz Butter
- 8oz Sugar
- 8oz Currants
- 8oz Raisins
- 4oz Mixed candied Peel
- 4oz Ground Almonds
- 1 Tub Glacé cherries (6oz)
- 4 Eggs
- Juice of 1 lemon and orange
- 1 Table spoonful of Baking Powder
- 3 Table Spoonfuls of Brandy

Christmas Cake

Grandma Sarah's

CAKES and BUNS

- Mix all the ingredients together thoroughly in a large bowl.

- Spoon the mixture into a lightly greased and lined, 8" round loose based caked tin and bake in a preheated oven at 180 °C/gas4/ fan oven 160 °C for 2/3 hrs.

- To test the cake mixture is cooked, insert a fine skewer into the cake - if it comes out clean then the cake is ready.

- Cool in the tin then turn out and decorate to your liking.

Christmas Cake

Grandma Sarah's CAKES and BUNS

- ¾ lb Plain Flour
- ½ lb Butter
- ½ lb Sugar
- ½ lb Currants
- ½ lb Raisons
- ¼ lb Mixed candied peel
- ¼ lb Ground almonds
- 1Tub of Glacé cherries (6 oz)
- 4 Eggs
- The juice of 1 lemon & 1 orange
- 1 Table spoonfuls of Brandy
- Bake for 2 to 3 hours

Christmas Cake

Grandma Sarah's CAKES and BUNS

- Mix all the ingredients together thoroughly in a large bowl.

- Spoon the mixture into a lightly greased and lined 8" round loose based cake tin and bake in a preheated oven at 180 °C/ gas 4/ fan oven 160*C for 2/3 hours.

- To test the cake mixture is cooked, insert a fine skewer into the cake – if it comes out clean then the cake is ready.

- Cool in the tin then turn out and decorate to your choice.

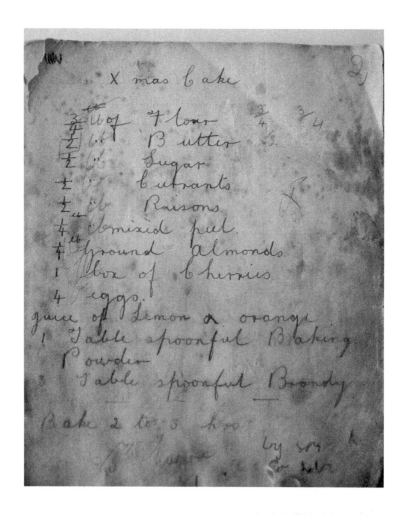

**Grandma Sarah's original Christmas cake recipe
in her original handwriting**

Date Cake

Grandma Sarah's CAKES and BUNS

- 5 Cupfuls of flour
- 1 ½ Cupfuls of sugar
- ½ lb of butter
- 1 Teaspoonful of carb soda (bicarbonate of soda)
- 8oz Dates
- 4 oz Walnuts
- 2 Teaspoonful of baking powder
- ¼ Pint boiling water
- Milk to mix

Place butter, sugar, dates, and bicarbonate of soda and walnuts together in a bowl add the boiling water mix well and leave to cool a little. Add the beaten egg, flour and baking powder and mix well combining all the ingredients thoroughly.

Date Cake

Grandma Sarah's CAKES and BUNS

- Pour into a lined 2lb loaf tin, and bake in a medium oven at 160°C/150°fan/gas mark 3 for 1 ¼ to 1 ½ hrs.

- Leave the cake to cool for about 10 to 15mins and carefully turn out on to a wire tray.

- Dredge with icing sugar and decorate with walnuts.

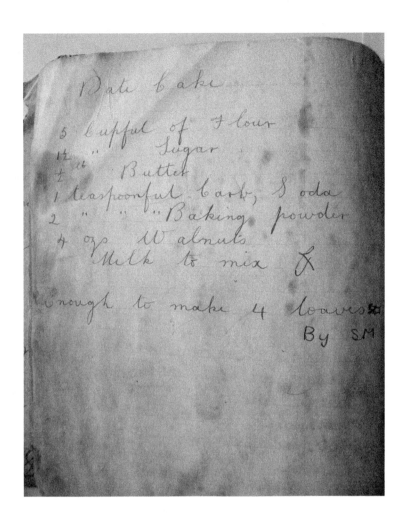

**Grandma Sarah's original date cake recipe
in her original handwriting**

Fruit Cake

Grandma Sarah's

CAKES and BUNS

When I saw Grandma Sarah's recipe for this fruit cake I was intrigued by the added ingredient of vinegar. I have found out that due to egg rationing during World War ll housewives used vinegar in place of eggs. Apparently vinegar makes cake batter more acidic, this has an effect on proteins in the flour making the cake fluffy yet moist. You don't have to eliminate egg just add a little vinegar to your next cake mixture to achieve the same effect.

Fruit Cake

Grandma Sarah's CAKES and BUNS

- 1lb/450g Flour
- 8ozs/225g Margarine/butter
- 6ozs/170g Currants
- 6ozs/170g Raisins
- 6ozs/170g Sugar
- ¼ Teasp of grated nutmeg /or 1teasp of ground nutmeg
- ½ Teasp mixed spice
- 1 or 2 eggs
- 1 ½ Tablespoons of vinegar
- 1 Teasp baking powder or 1 teasp baking soda mixed with 1 gill/ ¼ pint hot milk
- A little milk

Fruit Cake

Preheat the oven 150⁰C/gas 2

- Rub together the flour baking powder, sugar and the margarine until it resembles fine breadcrumbs and add the fruit and spices.

- If you are using the baking soda mix together with the hot milk and add to the dry ingredients (I used the baking powder and the cold milk) and mix well.

- Add the vinegar and mix well.

- Add the eggs, if the mixture seems too sloppy add only one egg.

- Pour into a greased and lined 2lb loaf tin or a 8" round tin and bake for 1 hour or until the cake feels firm , or the skewer comes out clean.

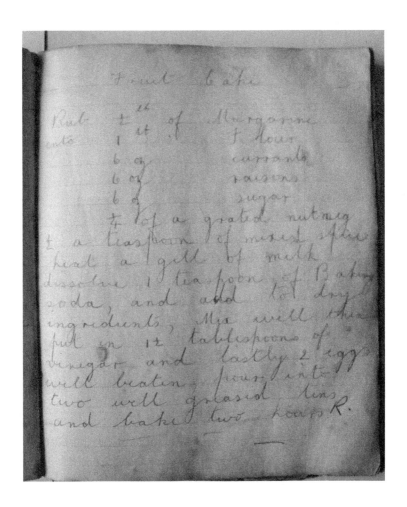

**Grandma Sarah's original fruit cake recipe
in her original handwriting**

Ginger Cake

Grandma Sarah's CAKES and BUNS

- ½ lb Flour
- 6 oz Margarine 2 teaspoonful of ginger
- 2 Teaspoonful of pudding spice
- 8 Dessert spoonfuls of sugar
- 2 Eggs
- Pinch of salt

- Mix all the dry ingredients together in a bowl, beat up the egg and add a little milk.

- Pour into a 2lb greased and lined loaf tin and bake for ¾ of an hour in a preheated moderate oven. Test by inserting a skewer in to the middle of the cake if it comes out clean then the cake is cooked. I should imagine that would be 160°C/150°F/gas mark 3.

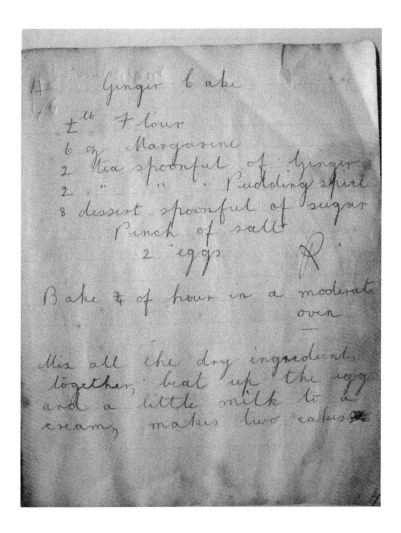

**Grandma Sarah's original ginger cake recipe
in her original handwriting**

Nelson Cake

Grandma Sarah's CAKES and BUNS

- 8ozs/225g S.R. Flour
- 4ozs/100g lard
- Hand full of sugar (3ozs)
- ½ Teasp salt
- 6ozs/160g Currants
- 100ml milk
- Grated peel of 1 lemon
- Preheat oven at 220°c/gas 7
- Soak the currants in water for about 15 minutes

This is a very easy and tasty cake to make. It was usually made in Grandma Sarah's day using all the bits of short crust pastry left over from other recipes made that day.

Nelson Cake

Grandma Sarah's CAKES and BUNS

Preheat oven at 220⁰c/gas 7

- Soak the currants in water for about 15 minutes.

- Using the rubbing in method, rub together the flour, salt and lard until the mixture resembles fine breadcrumbs.

- Add the milk little by little until mixture forms a stiff dough.

Nelson Cake

- Divide the dough in half, and roll one half out into a square to about ⅛inch thick and place onto a square sheet of grease proof paper.

- Drain the currants and scatter over the square of pastry, likewise with the sugar and the grated lemon peel and egg wash the edges of the pastry.

- Roll out the rest of the pastry as above to and place on the top of the other, and press down, egg wash and sprinkle with sugar.

- Trim the edges carefully leave about ¼ in from the edge of the paper taking care also not to tear the greaseproof paper or lining, making sure that it will fit into the tray or tin, carefully lift and place onto the baking tray or tin.

- Bake in the oven on the middle shelf for 15/20 until golden brown.

When cold cut into squares and serve on its own or with custard.

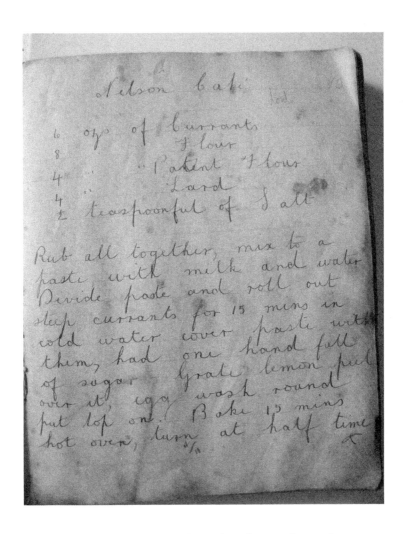

**Grandma Sarah's original Nelson cake recipe
in her original handwriting**

Madeira Cake

Grandma Sarah's CAKES and BUNS

- 6ozs/175g Butter
- 6ozs/175g Sugar
- 3 Eggs
- 9ozs/250g Self Raising Flour
- 2 Tablespoon milk
- 1 Teaspoonful Madeira wine, or essence
- The zest of 1 lemon
- 1-2 pieces of candied citron or lemon peel to decorate

Preheat the oven 180⁰C/350⁰F/gas 4

Madeira Cake

Grandma Sarah's

CAKES and BUNS

- Cream the butter and sugar together until the mixture is pale and creamy.
- Beat in the eggs one at a time.
- Fold in the flour gently until the mixture drops slowly off the spoon and fold in the lemon zest.
- Spoon the mixture into a 18cm/7" round cake tin.
- Bake in the middle shelf of the oven for 30/40mins until golden brown and a skewer inserted into the centre comes out clean.
- Remove from the oven and leave to cool in the tin for 10mins.
- Remove from the tin and place onto a wire rack and leave to cool completely.
- When cold, decorate the top with candied citron or lemon peel.

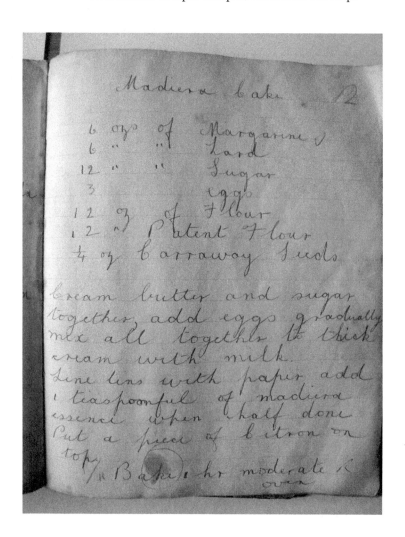

**Grandma Sarah's original Madeira cake recipe
in her original handwriting**

Parkin Cake

This is Grandma Sarah's recipe for Parkin which she made for many a Bonfire Night.

- 150g/6oz Oatmeal (or Porridge oats)
- 200g/6oz Self-raising flour
- 150g/4oz Brown sugar
- Dessert spoonful of ground Ginger
- 7 ozs/ 3 ½ Tablespoon of Treacle
- 7ozs/3 ½ Tablespoon Golden Syrup
- 150g/4oz Margarine or butter
- 1 Egg beaten

Parkin Cake

Grandma Sarah's CAKES and BUNS

Preheat the oven 150°C/gas 2/3

- Put all the dry ingredients into a large bowl and rub in the fat.

- Add the treacle, golden syrup and the egg and mix well. The mixture will be quite heavy.

- Pour into a lined tin.

Parkin Cake

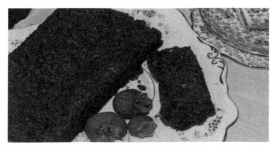

Bake in a slow oven for 1- 1 ½ hrs. Test the cake by inserting a skewer into the middle of the cake if comes out clean then the cake is ready, or if the cake is firm to touch then it is cooked. Leave in a cake tin for a minimum of two days before cutting and eating. The longer you leave Parkin the better it tastes.

Bonfire Night Celebrations in Great Britain.

Bonfire night also known as Guy Fawkes Night is celebrated primarily in Britain each year on the 5th of November.

In 1605 a group of English Catholics, conspired to blow up the Houses of Parliament along with the Protestant King James 1 of England, who was on the throne at the time, they wanted him replaced with a Catholic head of state.

Known as the *Gunpowder Plot*, the attempt failed and Guy Fawkes who was a member of the group was caught guarding a cache of explosives, he was arrested and sentenced to a traditional Traitors death, first by being tortured, then "hanged drawn and quartered" his body was then hacked into quarters and sent to the four corners of the kingdom as a warning to others.

Parkin Cake

Bonfire night became popular for working class children who gathered wood for the bonfire weeks before the 5th of November, they also made an effigy of Guy Fawkes to burn on the bonfire and the night became a street celebration for all, accompanied by, jaw breaking treacle toffee, Parkin and Fireworks and great vats of black peas.

Orange Cake

Grandma Sarah's CAKES and BUNS

- 8ozs/200g Self Raising flour
- 6ozs/150g Butter
- 6ozs/150g Sugar
- 2 Eggs
- ½ Teaspoon of baking powder
- Grated rind and the juice of one orange/ or tsp of orange essence
- Grease and line a 8 inch sandwich tin

Preheat oven 190C/gas 5

Orange Cake

- Sieve the flour, baking powder into a bowl and set aside.
- Cream the butter and sugar until pale and fluffy and a creamy consistency.
- Beat in each egg separately, adding a little of the flour if the mixture shows signs of curdling and add the rind and juice/ essence after the last egg.
- Fold in the rest of the flour.
- Spoon into the sandwich tins and bake for 30 mins or until the cake is firm to the touch.
- Do not open the oven when baking sponges until at least ¾ into the baking time.
- Cut in half when cold and spread with vanilla cream flavoured with a little orange essence and dust top with sieved icing sugar.

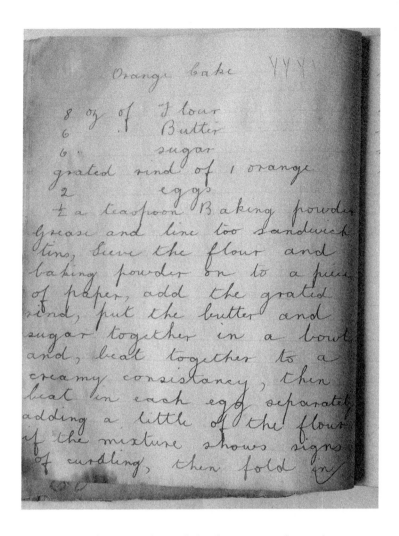

**Grandma Sarah's original orange cake recipe
in her original handwriting**

Short Cake

Grandma Sarah's CAKES and BUNS

- 6ozs/180g Plain Flour
- 2ozs/55g Castor Sugar
- 4ozs/125g Butter

Preheat the oven 180⁰C/gas 5

Short Cake

Grandma Sarah's CAKES and BUNS

- Cream the butter and sugar together until smooth.
- Stir in the flour until the mixture is a smooth paste.
- Turn out onto a work surface and gently roll out until the paste is 1cm or ½ " thick.
- Cut into shapes or fingers and leave to chill in the fridge for 20 minutes.
- Bake in the oven for 15-20 mins or until pale golden brown.
- Leave on the baking tray until cooled then transfer onto a wire cooling rack.

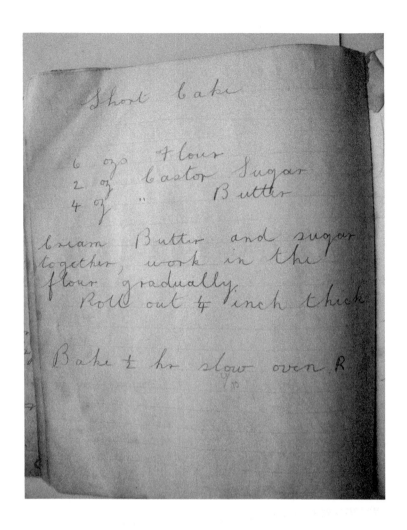

**Grandma Sarah's original short cake recipe
in her original handwriting**

Potato Cakes

This is one of my husbands favourite Grandma Sarah's recipes.

- 2lb Potatoes (buy the ones for mashing)
- ½ Teaspoon salt
- 1 Teaspoon Baking Powder
- 6ozs/180g Flour
- 4ozs/100g Lard

Preheat the oven to 250ºC/gas 9

Potato Cake

Grandma Sarah's POTATO CAKES

- Put the potatoes in a pan with enough water to just cover the top of them and bring to the boil, then simmer until soft.
- When cooked, drain the in a colander and return the potatoes to the pan, and mash using a potato masher or a fork.
- Leave to one side and allow to go cold.
- In a bowl rub the lard, flour, baking powder, and salt together and add the potatoes, and mix well until the mixture comes together and forms a fairly firm ball, add more flour if it's too soft to handle.
- Put a large spoonful of the potato mix onto a liberally floured surface, flour the rolling pin and roll gently or press into a circle, about ½ inch thick.

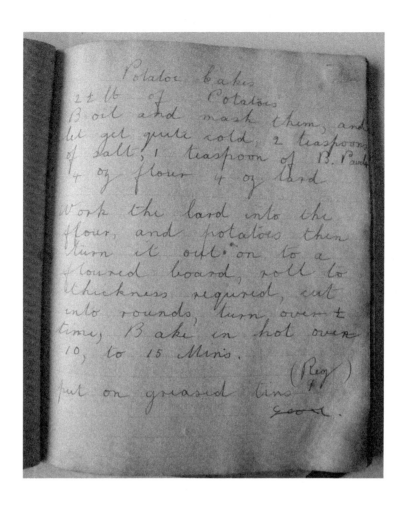

**Grandma Sarah's original potato cake recipe
in her original handwriting**

Queen Cakes

Grandma Sarah's CAKES and BUNS

- 4ozs/100g Butter
- 4ozs/100g Castor sugar
- 2 Eggs Beaten
- 4ozs/100g Self raising flour
- 2ozs/50g Currrants/Sultanas
- Teaspoon Lemon essence
- Tablespoon milk

Preheat the oven 190°C/gas 5

Queen Cakes

Grandma Sarah's CAKES and BUNS

- Cream the butter, and sugar together until pale and fluffy
- Beat in the eggs a little at a time
- Fold in the flour then add the fruit and mix well
- Fill the bun tray or paper cases half full with the mixture
- Bake for 15 mins or until golden brown
- Transfer onto a wire rack to cool

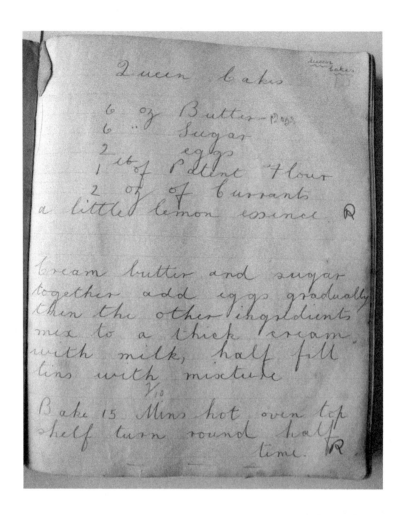

**Grandma Sarah's original Queen cake recipe
in her original handwriting**

Slab Cake

Grandma Sarah's CAKES and BUNS

- 6oz/170g Butter
- 6ozs/170g Sugar
- 2 Eggs
- 1 Teaspoon Baking Powder
- 10ozs/280g Self raising flour
- 6ozs/170g Raisins

Pre heat the oven to 180°C/gas 4

Slab Cake

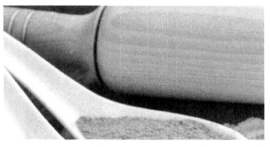

- Grease a square cake tin 8" by 10" or a loaf tin with butter, and line it with greaseproof paper.
- Cream the butter and sugar together until the mixture is light and creamy.
- Beat the eggs and add them gradually to avoid curdling.
- Mix well.
- Fold in the sifted flour gradually, then add the fruit mix well, and spoon the mixture into the tin.
- Sprinkle sugar onto the surface of the cake and decorate with Walnuts.
- Bake for 45-55 mins.
- Test the cake by inserting a skewer into the middle if it comes out clean the cake is cooked or until the cake feels springy.
- Leave to cool in the tin for 10mins before turning the cake out onto a wire cooling rack.

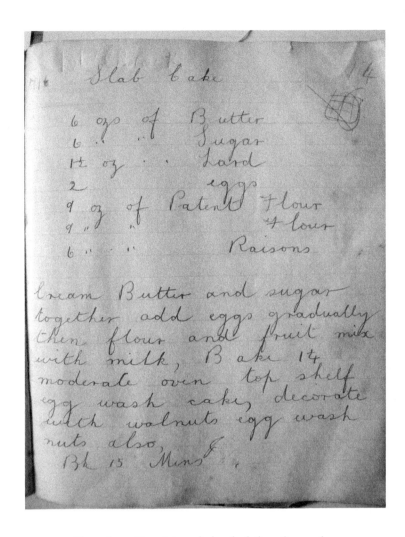

**Grandma Sarah's original slab cake recipe
in her original handwriting**

Wedding Cake

Grandma Sarah's CAKES and BUNS

- 2lbs of flour
- 10 Eggs
- 1lb of currants
- 1lb of raisins
- 1lb of butter
- 1lb of sugar
- ½lb Candied peel
- ¼ lb Angelica
- ¼ lb Ground Almonds
- 6d Essence of roses
- 1 Pinch of Carbonate of soda
- 1 Pinch of Cream of Tartar

Wedding Cake

Grandma Sarah's CAKES and BUNS

- In a large bowl, mix the eggs and the dry ingredients with a wooden spoon.
- Add the flour and mix well.
- Spoon all the mixture into a greased and lined 8/9" cake tin and bake on the middle shelf for 1hr 45min at 160°C or gas mark 3.
- Push a metal skewer in the centre of the cake, if it comes out clean then the cake is ready.
- Leave to cool in the tin and turn out onto a wire cooling tray and decorate to your own liking.

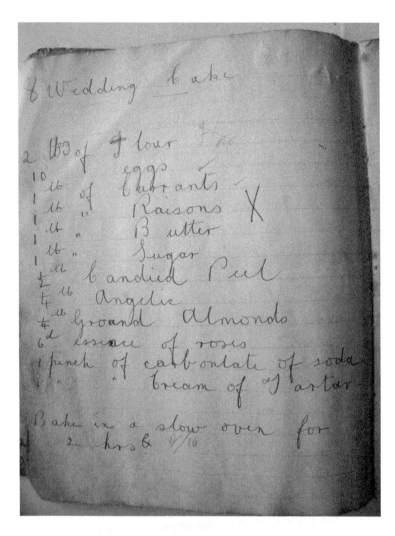

**Grandma Sarah's original wedding cake recipe
in her original handwriting**

Simnel Cake

Simnel Cake is traditionally eaten at Easter. In Mediaeval times young female servants would bake this rich fruit cake to take to their mothers on the rare visits home for Mothering Sunday. The Simnel Cake marked the end of the forty days of Lent in the Christian Calendar and the celebration of Easter time.

It is a delicious fruit cake, and I personally prefer it to Christmas cake, it is also a symbolic Easter Cake to signify Christianity. The 11 marzipan balls or figures, are placed around the edge of the cake represent the 11 disciples of Christ, although there were 12 apostles of Jesus Christ, Judas Iscariot betrayed him and hung himself so he is omitted. The slightly larger ball or figure in the centre of the cake signifies Jesus Christ.

This is Grandma Sarah's recipe for Simnel cake, I have converted the amounts as best I can and the cake was delicious.

Simnel Cake

Grandma Sarah's

CAKES and BUNS

- ¼ lb/100g Butter
- 2 Beaten eggs, and one for the glaze
- ¼ lb/100g Brown sugar
- 6oz/150 Plain flour
- ¼ lb/100g Raisins
- ¼ lb Currants
- 3ozs/80g Mixed Peel
- 1 Teaspoon of mixed spice
¼ Teaspoon bicarbonate of soda/ or baking powder
- 2 Tablespoons of milk or Orange Juice

Simnel Cake

- Almond Paste
- 6ozs/150g Ground Almonds
- 9oz /200g Castor Sugar
- 1 Egg
- Orange juice

Mix the sugar with the ground almonds, add the beaten egg and the orange juice little by little and mix to a stiff paste. Ready rolled marzipan is just as suitable to use.

To Make the cake

Preheat the oven to 140C/gas mark 1

- In a large bowl, cream the butter and sugar together until pale and fluffy.
- Slowly beat in the eggs and mix well.
- Divide the amount of flour into two and in one half, mix in the fruit and grated peel until all the fruit has a coating of flour, this helps stop the fruit from sinking to the bottom.

Simnel Cake

- Add the flour with the fruit and grated peel in and mix well.
- Fold in the rest of the flour and mix until all the ingredients are incorporated.
- Grease and line a 18cm tin and spoon half of the mixture into it and spread it smoothly in the tin.
- Using a third of the almond paste, roll out, to form a circle 18cm diameter and cover the cake mix with a layer of almond paste then add the remaining mixture making sure that it is evenly spread, leave a little dip in the centre to allow the cake to rise evenly.
- Place in the oven for 1 hour and thirty minutes (do not open the oven door for an hour).
- Test the cake by inserting a metal skewer into the centre of the cake, if it comes out clean then the cake is ready.
- Set aside to cool down.
- Brush the top of the cake with melted jam and place a circle of almond paste on the top and gently smooth down.
- From the remaining almond paste, make 11 balls and one slightly larger one and place these around the edge of the cake.
- Brush all the areas of almond paste with beaten egg and place in a preheated oven until the almond paste turns a light brown colour.

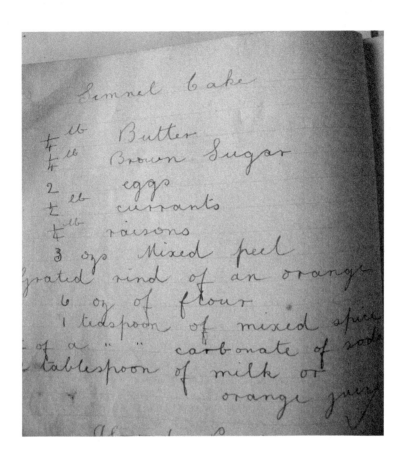

**Grandma Sarah's original simnel cake recipe
in her original handwriting**

Cake determined by weight of the egg

Grandma Sarah's CAKES and BUNS

To be honest when I saw this recipe I was doubtful as to whether it would work or not, but, once again Grandma Rules OK.

- 1 Egg
- It's weight in:
- Castor sugar
- Margarine/butter
- Ground Rice or rice flour
- Vanilla essence/almond essence
- Raspberry Jam

Preheat the oven to 180⁰C/gas 4/350F

Cake determined by weight of the egg

Grandma Sarah's CAKES and BUNS

First of all, line the bun tray or individual small tins with short crust pastry, put a small amount of jam on to the bottom of each of the pastry in the tins and set to one side.

- Cream the fat and the sugar to a cream, add the egg, and beat until smooth.
- Fold in the ground rice and essence and mix well.
- Spoon the mixture on top of the jam, careful not to over fill the bun cases.
- At this point I sprinkled flaked almonds over the top of each cake, but this is optional.
- Bake in the oven for 10-15 minutes until the cake is golden brown.

Rice Cake

Grandma Sarah's CAKES and BUNS

- 2oz ground rice
- ¼ lb flour
- 1 Teaspoonful baking powder
- 4oz caster sugar
- 1 Egg beaten
- Milk
- ¼ Butter and lard mixed
- Grated lemon rind

Rice Cake

- Put rice, flour and baking powder into a bowl and mix well.
- Rub in the butter and lard, add sugar and lemon rind and make into a light dough with egg and milk. Beat well and bake in a greased tin for ¾ hr.

Or:

- Cream the butter and the sugar together until pale and creamy.
- Add the egg and fold in all the other ingredients.
- Place into a loaf tin and bake in the middle of the oven at 170°C/fan 150°C.
- For 45mins/1hr .
- Leave to cool for 10mins before turning out onto a wire rack to cool completely.

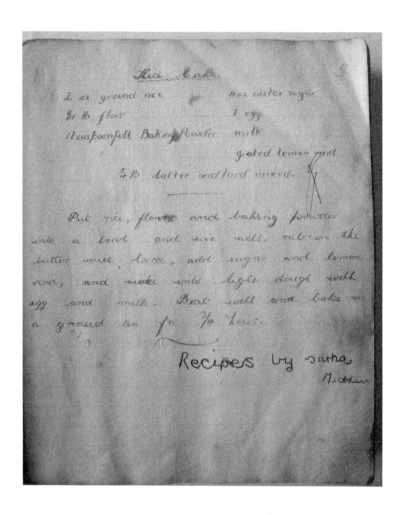

**Grandma Sarah's original rice cake recipe
in her original handwriting**

Swiss Roll

Grandma Sarah's CAKES and BUNS

- 2 Eggs
- 2oz of sugar
- 2 ½ oz of flour
- 1 Teaspoonful of baking powder

- Beat the eggs and sugar to a cream, add the flour and baking powder very gently and stir well together.
- Pour onto a greased and lined baking tray, spread the mixture into the corners of the baking tray with a spatula.

Bake in the centre of the oven for 10 to 12 mins at 160°C gas mark 3

Swiss Roll

Grandma Sarah's CAKES and BUNS

- Lay a clean damp tea towel on the work surface and cover the cloth with a piece of greaseproof paper larger than the sponge.
- Dust the greaseproof paper with caster sugar, run a knife around the warm sponge and carefully turn out onto the sugared paper.
- Peel off the original greaseproof off the base of the sponge and trim the edges so the sponge is nice and square.
- Spoon home-made jam and cream onto the sponge, leaving a little border all the way around and start to roll the sponge carefully.
- Leave seam down until cold.

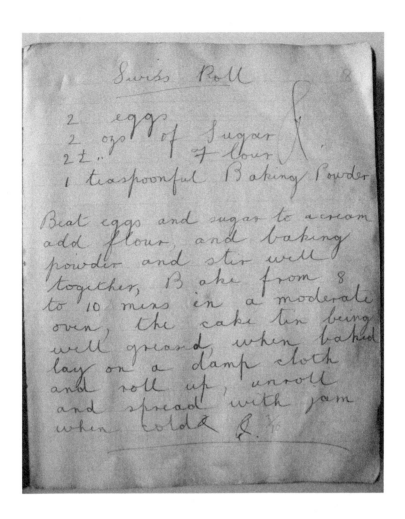

**Grandma Sarah's original Swiss roll recipe
in her original handwriting**

Cream Cake Puffs

Grandma Sarah's CAKES and BUNS

- 8 ozs /200g Puff pastry (recipe in the book or ready-made is fine)
- 1 Egg for glaze
- Lemon Cheese for filling
- Vanilla cream

Preheat oven to 150°C gas 4

- Roll out the puff pastry into an oblong shape.
- With a square cutter cut out shapes.
- Fold all the corners of the square shapes to the middle and brush with beaten egg wash.
- Bake for 15 mins until golden brown.
- When cool, fill the centre with lemon cheese (recipe in the book) and vanilla cream.

Ginger Sponge

Grandma Sarah's

CAKES and BUNS

- 3 Cups S.R. flour
- 1 Cup of sugar
- 1 ½ heaped teaspoonfuls ginger
- 1 Beaten egg
- ¼ lb margarine
- A good cup of milk
- 2 Tablespoons of black treacle or syrup.
- ½ Teaspoonful of bicarb mixed with a little of the milk

Ginger Sponge

Grandma Sarah's CAKES and BUNS

Rub in the flour, margarine, bicarb, sugar and ginger with your fingers until the mixture resembles breadcrumbs, add the beaten egg, milk, treacle or syrup and combine all the ingredients together.

- Pour into a lined 8"x8" cake tin.

- Bake in the middle of the oven at 180°C/gas mark 4 for 35 mins or until the sponge golden brown and is springy to the touch.

Tennis Cake

Grandma Sarah's CAKES and BUNS

- 2oz of Butter
- 2oz Sugar
- 1 Egg
- 4 oz Patent flour (SR flour is fine)
- ½ oz Chopped almonds
- ½ oz Candied peel
- 2 oz Currants or raisins
- ¼ Cupful of milk
- A little vanilla essence

Tennis Cake

Grandma Sarah's

CAKES and BUNS

- Cream the butter and sugar together, add the egg and mix well.
- Add the fruit nuts and candied peel and fold in the flour.
- Little by little add the milk until the mixture reaches a dropping consistency.
- Pour the mixture into a 7" loose bottom cake tin and bake in the middle of the oven at 180°C/gas mark 4 for 35 mins.
- Turn out onto a wire cooling rack and leave to cool before cutting into slices.

Victorian Sandwich

Grandma Sarah's CAKES and BUNS

- 8ozs/200g Self Raising Flour
- 4ozs/100g Butter
- 4ozs/100g Sugar
- 2 Eggs
- 3 Tablespoons of milk
- Lemon essence

Preheat oven to 150⁰C/gas 5
Line and grease 8" sandwich tin or use two 7" tins

- Cream the fat with a wooden spoon until soft.
- Add the sugar and beat until the mixture is light in colour and fluffy.
- Add the lemon essence.
- Add the eggs one at a time with a little of the sieved flour and mix well.
- Fold in the remaining flour.
- Spoon the mixture into the tin.
- And level with a palette knife or table knife.
- Bake for 25-30 mins or until the sponge feels firm to the touch.
- Leave in the tin for 10 mins.
- When cold, cut in half, spread with jam, sandwich together and dust the top with icing sugar.

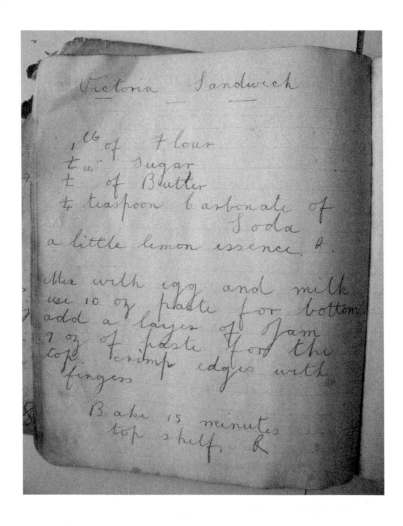

**Grandma Sarah's original Victorian sandwich recipe
in her original handwriting**

Russian Sandwich

- 4 ozs/100g sugar
- 4ozs/100g butter
- 2 Eggs
- 8ozs/200g Self raising flour

In this recipe Grandma Sarah uses lard and margarine, but I have used the equivalent in butter.

Preheat oven to 180C/gas4/350F

- Line an 8inch sandwich tin or two 7inch tins.
- Cream the butter and sugar until the mixture is light and fluffy.
- Add the eggs one at a time and mix well.
- Add the sieved flour gradually and spoon into the cake tins.
- Bake for 20 minutes until golden brown, test with a skewer that the cake is cooked.
- Turn onto a cooling rack and peel of the greaseproof paper.
- When cool cut in half and fill with vanilla cream (recipe in the book).
- Ice the top of the cake with pink water icing.
- Decorate by sprinkling coconut all around the edge of the cake.

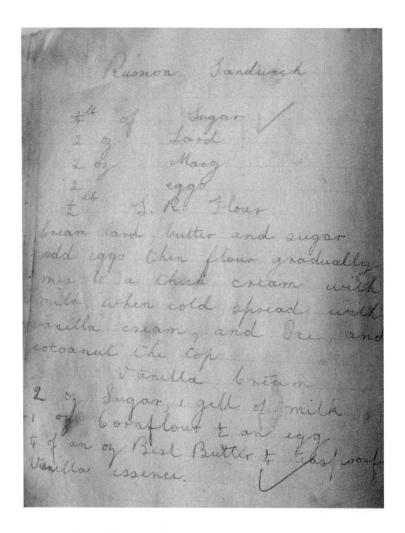

**Grandma Sarah's original Russian sandwich recipe
in her original handwriting**

Raspberry Sandwich

- ¼ lb /100g Sugar
- ¼ lb 100g Flour
- 2ozs /50g Butter warm (I think she means room temperature)
- 1 Egg
- 2 Tablespoons of water
- 2 Drops of essence of Lemon
- 1 Teaspoon of baking powder

Preheat the oven to 160⁰C/gas3

- Cream the butter and sugar together until the mixture is light and creamy, add the lemon essence.
- Add the eggs one by one and mix until smooth.
- Fold in the sifted flour and baking powder.
- The mixture should drop of the spoon easily if it is too stiff add the water.
- Divide into two greased and lined 8" sandwich tins, and smooth out with a spatula.
- Place in the centre of the oven and bake for 30/35 mins.

DO NOT OPEN THE OVEN DOOR UNTIL 30 mins HAS ELAPSED.

Raspberry Sandwich

Grandma Sarah's
CAKES and BUNS

- Test if the cake is ready by inserting a metal skewer into the centre if it comes out clean then the cake is ready.

- Leave for about 1 minute before turning out onto a wire cooling tray and peel off the greaseproof paper.

- When cold, spread raspberry jam/whipped cream over one of the cakes and place the other on top.

- Dust with icing sugar and decorate with raspberries before serving.

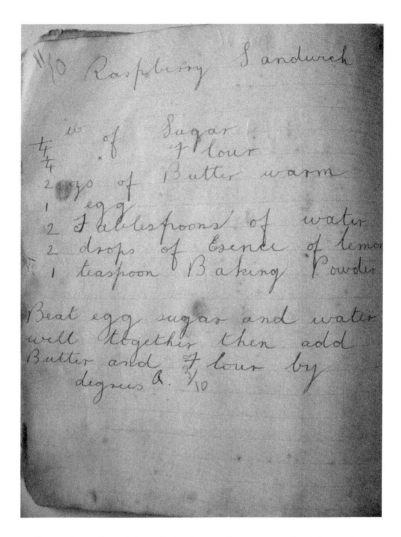

**Grandma Sarah's original raspberry sandwich recipe
in her original handwriting**

Grandma Sarah's
Bread

*The quantities listed are far too large for today's needs. Grandma Sarah probably made her bread in batches of this size to utilise the temperature of the oven, and therefore have bread in store in the pantry for quite a few days. My advice to you would be to use ¼ of the amounts listed in this section.

Brown Bread

Grandma Sarah's BREAD

- Brown Bread
- 6lb of Wheat Flour
- 2lb of Plain Flour
- 2oz of salt
- 3oz of balm.
- ½ pt of warm water

In this recipe the terminology is slightly different to the recipe for bread-making of today, for instance, Grandma Sarah mentions wheatmeal? This is what we know as wholemeal flour, and she also mentions balm? This is what we know as yeast. In those days fresh yeast was always used, my mother also only used fresh yeast, in my opinion it produces a better softer bread although the dried yeasts used today are very popular.

- Rub together, knead to a light dough, with warm water, tin at once, let it rise until double its size.

In other words:

- In a large warm bowl put the flour and the salt , make a well in the middle.In a cup, mix the yeast with a teaspoon of sugar stir until together until it liquefies, then add ¼pt of luke warm water.

Brown Bread

- Pour into the well in the middle of the bowl and cover with a cloth and leave to ferment for about 5/10 minutes until the liquid in the middle had started to bubble and foam.
- Mix together all the ingredients together until a soft stretchy dough is formed.
- Turn out onto a clean lightly floured surface and knead the bread dough until it is smooth and no longer sticky. (for about 10 minutes).
- Divide the dough into the sizes required for loaves and rolls and place into tins and onto baking trays, cover with a damp tea towel and leave to rise until the bread has doubled in size.
- Bake in a preheated oven at 200°C/400F°/gas6 for 30/40 mins.
- To test if the bread is cooked, turn the loaves out of the tins and return to the oven and bake for a further 10 mins to bake the base and the sides.

Test by tapping the base of the bread if it sounds hollow then the bread is cooked.

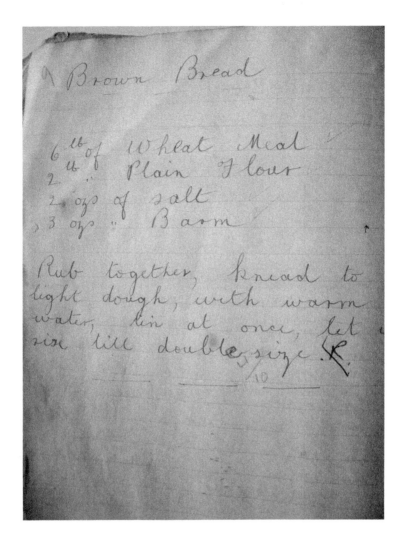

**Grandma Sarah's original brown bread recipe
in her original handwriting**

White Bread

- 1 ½ lbs Strong White Bread flour
- 2 teasp salt (do not let the salt come in direct contact with the yeast or it will kill it)
- 1 teasp sugar
- 15g of fresh yeast
- 14 fluid ounces/400ml luke warm water

Preheat oven to 200⁰C/gas 6

- In a large warm bowl put the flour and the salt , make a well in the middle. In a cup, mix the yeast with a teaspoon of sugar stir until together until it liquefies, then add ¼pt of luke warm water.

- Pour into the well in the middle of the bowl and cover with a cloth and leave to ferment for about 5/10 minutes until the liquid in the middle had started to bubble and foam.

- Mix together all the ingredients together until a soft stretchy dough is formed.

White Bread

Grandma Sarah's BREAD

- Turn out onto a clean lightly floured surface and knead the bread dough until it is smooth and no longer sticky. (for about 10 minutes).

- Divide the dough into the sizes required for loaves and rolls and place into tins and onto baking trays, cover with a damp tea towel and leave to rise until the bread has doubled in size.

- Bake in a preheated oven at 200°C/400F°/gas6 for 30/40 mins.

- To test if the bread is cooked, turn the loaves out of the tins and return to the oven and bake for a further 10 mins to bake the base and the sides. Test by tapping the base of the bread if it sounds hollow then the bread is cooked.

White Bread

Grandma Sarah's BREAD

- Divide the dough into the sizes required for loaves and rolls and place into tins and onto baking trays, cover with a damp tea towel and leave to rise until the bread has doubled in size.

- Bake in a preheated oven at 200°C/400F°/gas6 for 30/40 mins.

- To test if the bread is cooked, turn the loaves out of the tins and return to the oven and bake for a further 10 mins to bake the base and the sides. Test by tapping the base of the bread if it sounds hollow then the bread is cooked.

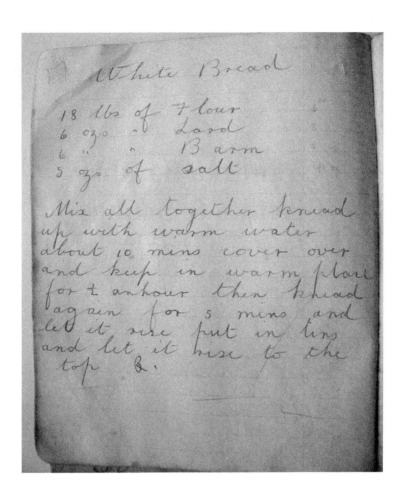

**Grandma Sarah's original white bread recipe
in her original handwriting**

Grandma Sarah's
Biscuits & Scones

Shortbread Bicuits

Grandma Sarah's

BISCUITS and SCONES

- 1lb of flour
- 10 ozs of margarine
- 6 ozs of sugar
- Pinch of salt
- 1 or 2 cherries

Mix to a stiff dough, roll out ½ inch thick. Cut out into shapes.

Method

-Cream together the sugar and the margarine, gradually add the flour and the fruit and form the mixture into a smooth ball.

- Roll out to about 2" thick and cut into shapes, place on a baking tray and cook for about 12 mins at 190 deg C. Or until pale brown.

The biscuits will appear soft when you lift them from the baking tray, but will harden up when cool.

Scones

Grandma Sarah's BISCUITS and SCONES

- 1lb/ 450g Flour
- 1 tsp of baking powder
- 3oz/85g sugar
- 2oz/50g currants
- 2oz/50g sultanas
- 4oz/100g butter
- Breakfast cup/100ml of milk
- 1 Egg

Preheat the oven at 200⁰ C

- In a large bowl, put the flour, baking powder and the butter.
- Rub in the flour and butter until the mixture resembles fine bread crumbs.
- Add the dried fruit and sugar and egg and mix, adding the milk little by little until the mixture forms a firm dough and the dough leaves the sides of the mixing bowl and forms a ball.
- Turn out on to a floured surface and roll out or press the dough gently with your hand until it is about 1 ½ /38mm thick.
- Select the cutter and cut out the scones and place on a lightly floured or greased baking tray. Brush the top of the scones with milk.
- Bake for 12/15 mins or until the scones are golden brown.
- When cold, cut the scones in two, fill with jam and clotted cream.
- Then put the top half onto the bottom half and serve.

Grandma Sarah's Antique Recipes

Grandma Sarah's
Pudding

Christmas Pudding

- 2oz/50g Suet/Vegetarian Suet
- 6oz/170g Flour
- 1 Teaspoon Baking Powder
- 4oz/100g Currants
- 2oz/50g   Raisins
- 1oz/25g Candied Peel
- 2oz/50g Sugar
- 1 Dessert spoon of Black treacle
- 1 Teaspoon of Mixed Spice
- 2 Eggs
- A little milk for mixing
- 100 ml Brandy.

- Grease the pudding bowl/ deep cereal bowl, or microwave or heat -proof bowl, well, with butter and set to one side.
- In a large mixing bowl mix together all the ingredients and stir well, add a little milk to the mixture if it feels too dry.
- Transfer the mixture into the pudding bowl.
- Draw round a dinner plate and cut a circle out of greaseproof paper to cover the top of the bowl, and secure with an elastic band.

Christmas Pudding

To Steam:
- Place in a large pan of boiling water and steam for 1 hr or until the pudding feels firm on the top.

To Microwave:
- Cook in the microwave for 5 mins until the top of the pudding feels firm.
- Carefully remove from the pan/microwave and peel off the greaseproof paper.
- Turn out onto a serving plate and serve with clotted cream or brandy butter.

Tony's Pudding

Grandma Sarah's PUDDING

- ¼ lb/4ozs/100g orange marmalade
- 3 Sponge fingers/cakes
- 1 Pint of milk
- 2 Eggs/ separate yolks from white
- 1 Teaspoon / 2ozs of sugar

Preheat oven 150C/gas 2/300F

Sultana Pudding

Grandma Sarah's PUDDING

- 6 Tablespoons of flour
- 4 Tablespoons of suet
- 3 Tablespoons of sugar
- 3 Tablespoons of sultanas
- ½ Teaspoonful of carbonate of soda

- Boil one cupful of milk and pour over the soda, add all the other ingredients and mix well until the mixture resembles a thick batter.

Sultana Pudding

Grandma Sarah's PUDDING

- Put into a large pudding basin.
- In a large pan add 1 ½ litres of water and bring to a simmer.
- Cover the top of the basin with greaseproof paper, put a saucer on top and tie up securely in a tea towel.
- Place in the pan of simmering water, making sure that the water is no higher than halfway up the sides of the basin, and boil for 2 ½ to 3 hrs.
- Remove the tea towel and the greaseproof paper, and run a knife carefully around the edges of the basin.
- Turn out onto a plate and eat with lashings of custard.

Grandma Sarah's
Sweets

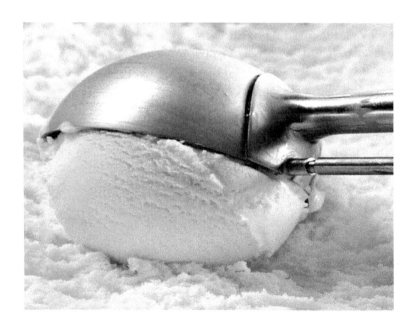

Vanilla Ice Cream

- 1 pint milk/cream or half and half
- 4ozs/ 100g Sugar
- 2 eggs/2 egg yolks
- 2 Tablespoons cornflour (2ozs)
- 1 Teaspoon vanilla essence / vanilla pod

This recipe is a lovely filling for all sorts of cakes and pastries I have adapted Grandma Sarah's recipe to make a larger amount:

- Put the milk in a saucepan and place it on the cooker on a medium heat and let it come almost to the boil.
- In a separate bowl add the sugar, eggs and cornflour and whisk thoroughly.
- Add the hot milk to the above little by little stirring all the time, until all the hot milk is added.
- Return the mixture from the bowl to the pan and return to the cooker on a low heat, stirring all the time.
- Do not hurry this stage or you will end up with scrambled eggs.
- The mixture will slowly start to thicken add the vanilla essence and keep stirring.
- When the custard mixture is thick transfer it into a bowl and cover with cling film (this will stop a skin forming on the custard) and place in the fridge to chill.
- Once it is chilled it is ready to use as you wish.

Coconut Cones

- 8ozs/ 225g Desiccated Coconut
- 6ozs/ 150g Sugar
- 1 Egg beaten
- Glace cherries to decorate/ or drizzle with chocolate

Preheat oven 180⁰C gas 4

- Lightly grease a baking tray and set to one side.
- Beat the eggs and add the coconut and sugar, if the mix is a little stiff add a little milk.
- Moisten an egg cup with milk and fill it with the coconut mixture.
- Turn out onto the baking tray and bake for 25/30 mins or until golden brown.
- Leave to cool on a wire rack and decorate with cherries or dip the tops in melted chocolate.

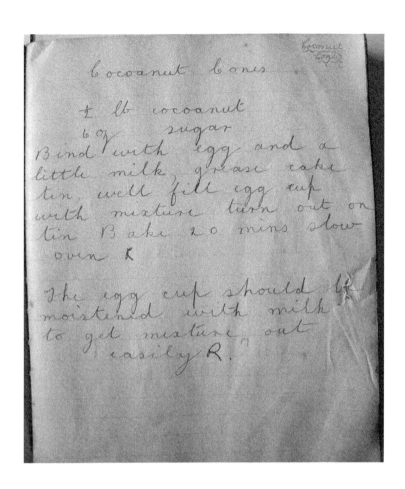

**Grandma Sarah's original coconut cones recipe
in her original handwriting**

Coconut Ice

- 200g Condensed milk
- 8ozs/225g Icing sugar
- 8ozs/225g Desiccated coconut
- 1 Tiny drop of natural red food colouring

- Line a small plastic box with cling film or greaseproof paper.
- Mix together the icing sugar and condensed milk and the coconut (the mixture should be very stiff) keep mixing until all the condensed milk is absorbed.
- Divide the mixture into two.
- Place half of the mix into the plastic box and press down firmly to form the base.
- Colour the other half of the coconut mix with food colouring until it is pale pink, keep mixing until you have an even colour.
- Place the pink coconut on top of the white coconut base and press firmly together.
- Leave to set in the fridge for 2-3 hours.
- Turn out of the box and cut into squares.
- Keep in the fridge in an airtight container and use within 3 weeks.

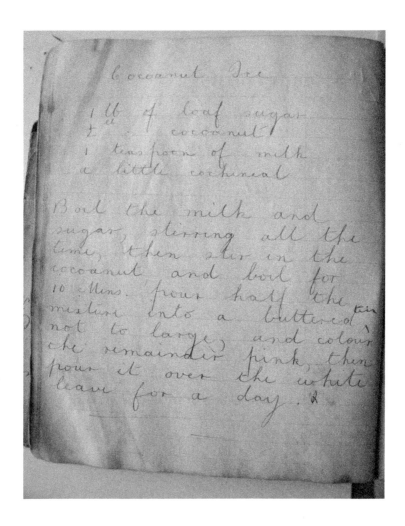

**Grandma Sarah's original raspberry coconut ice recipe
in her original handwriting**

This recipe is so easy to make, children can make it as a present for Christmas or birthdays. The Coconut Ice squares look so appealing and delicate when put in their own individual wrapper and presented in an attractive box or Jar.

Cream Horns

For this recipe you will need:

- Cream horn metal cones
- 1 Sheet/ Pkt of frozen puff pastry (thawed)
- Castor sugar for dusting
- Whipped Cream
- Glace cherries for decoration or fresh fruit of your choice
- 1 Egg
- 1 Teaspoon of water
- 1 Tablespoon of sugar

Preheat the oven 200C/400F/gas6

- Grease the metal cones with butter and set to one side.
- Roll out the puff pastry to an oblong as long as possible about ⅛ of an inch thick.
- Cut the dough lengthwise into 1 inch wide strips.
- Wind the strips around the greased cone starting at the point of the cone first, overlapping the layers slightly all the way to the top, do not wind them too tightly.

I have found that if you can wrap and cover each cone with one long strip of pastry the results are much better.

Cream Horns

Grandma Sarah's

SWEETS

- Place cones on sealed side down on a baking sheet and chill for 20 minutes (they can be frozen for later use at this stage in an airtight container).
- When ready to bake whisk the egg with the water, and lightly brush the pastry.
- Shake a little castor sugar on to a sheet of grease proof paper and roll the cones in the sugar until covered.
- On a baking tray covered with greaseproof paper or parchment paper place them seam side down and bake for about 20 mins until golden brown.
- Let them cool before removing them from the metal cones.
- Whip the cream with the tablespoon of sugar until stiff.
- Pipe the cream into the cones until full to the top, and decorate with fruit.

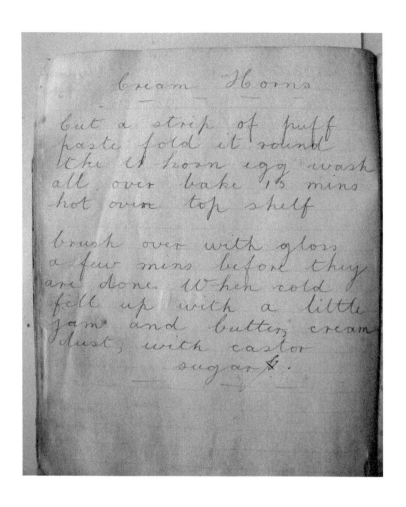

**Grandma Sarah's original cream horns recipe
in her original handwriting**

Lemon Curd Cream

Grandma Sarah's SWEETS

- 2ozs/ 50g Butter
- 3ozs/75g Icing sugar
- 1 ½ tablespoons of lemon curd.

- Beat the margarine until soft.
- Add the sugar and beat to a cream.
- Stir in the lemon curd gradually and beat again.
- Use a filling to cream cake puffs.

Cosies

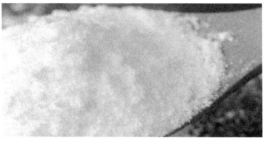

Grandma Sarah's

SWEETS

- 4ozs/100g Butter
- 3ozs/80g sugar
- 1 Egg
- 8ozs/220g Self raising flour
- ½ Teaspoon Baking powder
- Lemon essence
- 1oz coconut
- Raspberry Jam
- Square 8" tin

Preheat oven to 180⁰C/gas 5
- Cream the butter and sugar together until the mixture is creamy add the lemon essence.
- Add the egg little by little.
- Fold in the flour and mix well.
- Spoon into the tin and bake in the oven for 20/30 mins or until the sponge is golden and firm to the touch.

TIP: Do not open the oven door before 20mins or the cake will sink in the middle.
- When cooked remove from the oven and put to cool on a wire cooling tray.
- When cold cut into squares and spread with jam and dip in the coconut and serve.

Christmas Mincemeat

- 2oz/50g Shredded suet or vegetarian suet
- 4oz/100g Apples cored and chopped into small pieces.
- 4oz/100g Raisins
- 4oz/100g Currants
- 4oz/100g Sultanas
- 4oz/100g Candied or mixed peel
- 3oz/75g Demerara Sugar

- Teaspoonful of nutmeg or ¼ of a whole nutmeg grated.
- Teaspoonful mixed spice.
- Juice and zest of 2 oranges.
- 100ml of either brandy, rum or port.
- In a large bowl put the suet, dried fruit, sugar and apples, spices and mix well.
- Add the orange juice and alcohol and stir until all the contents are all combined.
- Spoon into screw top sterilised jam jars, seal and screw on the lid.
- Leave in the fridge overnight to allow all the flavours to infuse.
- Mincemeat will keep for 2-3 weeks in a cool place.

Treacle Toffee

- 1 Pound (500g) castor sugar
- ¼ Pound (125g) butter
- 1 Dessert spoon treacle
- 3 Dessert spoons golden syrup (dip the spoon into boiling water first and the syrup and treacle will just slide off)
- 1 Teaspoon vanilla essence
- Large tin condensed milk
- 5 or 6 dessert spoons water

- Grease and line a baking tray or square cake tin with greaseproof paper or parchment.

- Place the butter, sugar, treacle, syrup and water into a pan and heat, stirring constantly. When all the ingredients are well mixed and melted, add the condensed milk slowly, stirring occasionally until it boils.

- Continue on a slow boil for 15-20 minutes, again stirring occasionally. Test that the toffee is ready by dropping a spoonful into dish with ice cubes and cold water - if the toffee turns solid, it is ready to pour into the tin.

Treacle Toffee

Grandma Sarah's SWEETS

- Pour into a tray, leave for 10mins to set a little, and mark out with a knife and cut into pieces when set.

- Store in an air-tight container.

- Please have a bowl of very hot soapy water ready to soak all the utensils immediately after use.

This will help enormously when you come to wash up.

Lemon Cheese

There are a few variations of this recipe in the book, all of them intrigue me especially the terminology.

- **Lemon Cheese**
- **1 Large lemon**
- **1 Egg, well beaten**
- **1 Tea cup of sugar,**
- **1 Piece of butter, size of a walnut**
- **2 Tablespoons of water**
- **1 Teaspoonful of cornflour mix to a paste with water**

Start by whisking the eggs in a saucepan and then add all the other ingredients. Place the pan on a medium heat and keep whisking all the ingredients until the mixture stars to thicken. (7 or 8 mins) turn the stove down to the lowest heat, and simmer for a further minute whisking all the time.

Ladle into warm clean jars and seal. Leave to cool and then label and date.

**Grandma Sarah's original lemon cheese recipe
in her original handwriting**

Brandy Snaps

- 4ozs/100g Flour
- 4ozs/ Syrup (2 rounded tablespoons)
- 4ozs/100g sugar
- 4ozs/100g butter
- Juice of half a lemon
- 25mls Brandy / or teaspoon brandy essence/ ¼ teasp ginger

Preheat oven to 170⁰C/ gas 3

- Lightly grease a non-stick baking tray.

- Put the butter/margarine, sugar, lemon juice and brandy flavour into a saucepan and melt them slowly on a very slow heat.

Brandy Snaps

- Sieve flour, and if you are using ginger add it at this stage along with the flour and add the flour and ginger to the pan.

- On a low heat, warm the mixture gently but do not cook, stirring all the time.

- Remove from the heat and put teaspoons of the mixture onto a well greased baking tray, making sure that each spoonful of mixture are 3" ins apart as they will spread.

- Cook for 10/12 min until they are nicely brown.

- Leave to cool for about 30 secs, before removing them from the tin.

- Quickly take them off the tray, turn them over and quickly roll them around the handle of a wooden spoon. This bit has to be done quickly whilst the snaps are warm and pliable.

- When cold fill with brandy/rum butter or clotted cream or eat them just as they are.

Brandy Snaps

Brandy/Rum Butter

- 4ozs/100g Butter
- 3ozs/75g Sugar
- Rum or Brandy to taste
- Beat the butter and sugar to a cream add the brandy or rum to taste

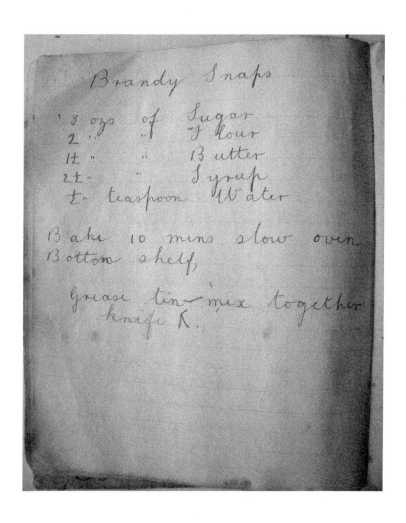

**Grandma Sarah's original brandy snaps recipe
in her original handwriting**

Grandma Sarah's Potato Pie

Potato Pie

This recipe is a stock Lancashire dish, it has been made for decades and is still popular today. It's a tasty filling meal and it was very economical and popular with mothers with large families. The recipe below will make 1 large pie on 4 smaller ones:
8oz/ 250g Grandma Sarah's Short crust Pastry (recipe in the book).

- **2/3 lbs of potatoes**
- **1 Large onion**
- **1 Pint of hot beef stock   (or beef stock cubes)**
- **1lb/ 500g Best Lean minced beef/steak**
- **Salt and pepper to season**

Preheat oven 180⁰C/gas mark3

- Peel potatoes and cut into small pieces and set aside.
- Roughly chop the onion and set aside.
- In a large pan cook the meat until brown and add the onions, potatoes and hot stock and stir.
- Bring to the boil and turn down to a simmer for 10mins stirring the pan from time to time.

Potato Pie

Grandma Sarah's

POTATO PIE

- While the pie mixture is simmering, roll out the pastry to fit the top of the dish and set to one side.

- Take the pan off the cooker and stir thoroughly, then carefully, spoon the hot mix into the dish and fill to the top.

- Carefully lay the pastry on top of the pie and press the edges down around the dish.

- Brush with egg wash and cook for 30mins.

- Serve with mushy peas, red cabbage or pickles of your choice.

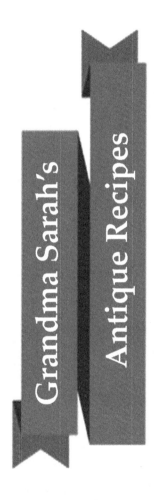

Grandma Sarah's
Sausage Rolls

Sausage Rolls

This is the easiest sausage roll recipe I have ever made.

Packet Puff pastry (easier to use and more economical)

- 2 Large Sausage (Buy the best quality available)
- 1 Thick slice of bread.
- Salt/pepper
- Egg wash

Preheat oven 200⁰C/400F/gas 6

- Soak the bread in 50ml of water and set aside.
- Slit the sausage at the side and peel off the skin.
- In a bowl, put the sausage and add the seasoning.
- Squeeze the water out of the bread and add it to the sausage.
- Mix well and set aside.
- Divide the puff pastry in two and roll out one half in the shape of an oblong and egg wash all around the edges.
- Take a spoonful of sausage mix and make a long sausage shape along the top of the oblong of pastry leaving ¼ in from the edge. well.

Sausage Rolls

- Mark around the edges with a fork, and make two small cuts in the top to allow steam to escape.

- Repeat the above until all the sausage meat is used.

- Bake in the oven for 10-15mins until the rolls are nice and brown.

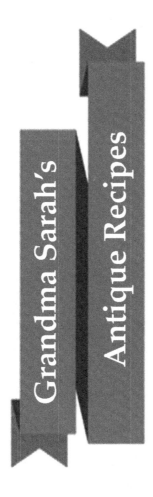

Grandma Sarah's Shortcrust Pastry

Shortcrust Pastry

Grandma Sarah's

SHORTCRUST PASTRY

- 8oz Plain flour
- 4oz lard
- Pinch salt
- 100 ml water

- Put the flour, salt and lard into a bowl and rub the flour and the lard together until the mixture resembles breadcrumbs.
- Add the water steadily and mix together with a knife until the pastry begins to form a ball and all the mixture comes clean away from the sides of the bowl.
- Turn out onto a floured surface and divide into required amounts.
- Leave in the fridge for about 20mins before using or wrap in cling film and freeze until needed.

Tip: Shortcrust pastry responds much better to cool conditions, i.e. metal bowl, mix with a cold metal knife. Cool in the fridge before using.

Grandma Sarah's Drinks

Ginger Wine

- 2d of essence of Ginger (10ml) maybe?
- 1d of essence of raspberry (5ml) maybe?
- 1d of essence of cayenne (5ml) maybe?
- ½ oz of tartaric acid
- 2 Quarts of water (4 pints)
- 1 lb of sugar

I should imagine the method used for this recipe is the same as the lemonade recipe? Adding the tartaric acid last. This recipe for Ginger Wine is very different to the one I am familiar with and I'm not quite sure how it would taste.

Although I have endeavoured to convert and modify most of Grandma Sarah's recipes I must admit that this has me stumped.

In this recipe I'm not sure what a pennorth or tuppenyworth of anything would equate to so I have written as I see and used my own idea for the method.

**Grandma Sarah's original ginger wine recipe
in her original handwriting**

Lemonade

- The juice and the zest of 2 large lemons
- 4oz/100g Sugar
- 100ml water.
- 1 Litre of refrigerated soda water or fizzy mineral water

- Grate the zest of the lemons into a container, cut the lemons in half and squeeze out all the juice and add to the zest and stir.
- In a small pan add the water and the sugar and put on a medium heat, stirring all the time, until the sugar has melted.
- Continue stirring on a medium but gentle heat, until the mixture thickens and becomes a light syrup.
- Do not allow the syrup to turn brown.
- When the syrup is ready take it off the heat and set aside.
- Strain the lemon mixture to get rid of the pips and add it to the syrup mixture in the pan.
- Into a large Jug, Pour the syrup and lemon mixture into a large jug add to it the chilled soda water and stir well.
- Bottle it and seal tightly.

Or serve immediately with slices of lemon?/lime and ice.

Lemonade

- 6 to 8 Large lemons
- 2 oz's Citric acid
- 2lb Sugar
- 1 ½ Pints of boiling water

- Grate the rind of the lemons.
- Add the sugar and citric acid.
- Pour on the boiling water.
- Add the juice of the remaining lemons.
- Stir well and strain.
- Allow to cool.
- Pour into a large jug or bottle.
- The citric acid is replaced today by soda water or mineral water.

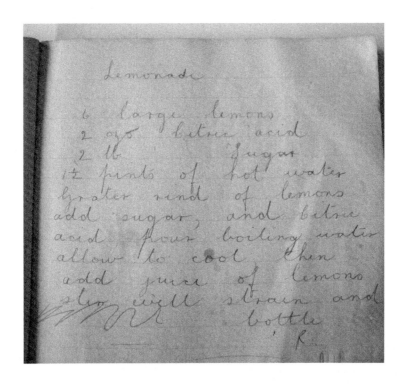

**Grandma Sarah's original homemade lemonade recipe
in her original handwriting**

Grandma Sarah's Remedies

Medicines & Cures

Medicines and cures from a Bygone Age

Before the National Health Service was introduced in 1948, research shows that for most people it was difficult to afford medicines.

Visiting a doctor in the early 1900's was expensive and for the working class a doctors fee was out of the question unless it was absolutely necessary.

For working class families, medicines handed down by family members would be the first choice, they were tried and tested remedies and people were able to buy the raw ingredients from their local chemist.

The chemists shelves were filled with ingredients to make all kinds of remedies and cures, and they were affordable for most working class people.

Here are some of the remedies passed down to Grandma Sarah for her to use.

A Good Tonic (1)

In a pan or Jug add:

- 1 Bottle of raisin wine
- 1 Gill of black beer
- 2oz of Bovril
- 1 Teaspoon of ammoniated citrate of iron

- Melt the iron in a little hot water then put in the Bovril, wine and beer.

- Transfer into a bottle, this makes about a quart.

Grandma Sarah does not state the dosage but I would imagine it would be a dessert spoonful after meals.

Blood Pressure

Grandma Sarah's REMEDIES

I'm not sure whether this medicine is for high or low blood pressure, not only that, how did people know if they had either?

- **1 oz Vervain Root**
- **1 oz Valerion**
- **1oz Scull cap**
- **1oz Mistletoe**

- Mix together and then divide into 4 equal parts and make up to 1 pint for each part.

Grandma Sarah doesn't say what the above is mixed with to make up the volume of 1 pint for each part I can only assume it is with water?

A Good Tonic (2)

- 1oz Hypophosphites
- 1oz Chemical Food
- 1oz Extract of malt

Dosage:

Then fill up with cold water? (to what amount she doesn't say) and take one dessertspoonful after meals.

Once again Grandma Sarah would be familiar with these cures, they must have been used by the family on a regular basis, and the need for detail is sometimes left out.

Cough Mixture

I do not know the equivalent amount in metric of 2d (two pennorth) of anything would be, although I can remember buying 2d of sweets as a child. The amount of tuppence (2d) is a unit of what was then known as a shilling, and there were 12 pennies in the old imperial shilling. Therefore 2d would be a ⅙ unit of a shilling. The equivalent financial value of a shilling in today would be 5p.

Cough Mixture:

- 2d   **Oil of aniseed**
- 2d   **Peppermint**
- 2d   **Laudanum**
- 2d   **White vinegar**
- 2oz **Spanish**
- 1lb **Black Treacle**

Boil the treacle and Spanish in a quart of water and reduce down to a pint, when cold, add the other ingredients and then bottle.

Dose: One Tablespoon in two tablespoons of warm water.

Nerve Tonic

- ½ oz **Valerian Root**
- ½ oz **Sarsaparilla Root**
- ½ oz **Camomile Flowers**
- ½ oz **Mistletoe Leaves**
- ½ oz **Scull Cap**

Will make 2 qrts, brewed twice?
Taken at night and morning.

Grandma Sarah's REMEDIES

Grandma Sarah does not state how this tonic is made up, nor is she clear on the dosage.

Most of these cures have been handed down by family from a long time ago so, by writing that the above ingredients will make a quantity of 2 quarts of liquid and stating the word Brewed, I can only guess that the above Nerve tonic was made up with water and drank as some sort of tea, but I couldn't be at all sure of this.

Stomach Bottle

Grandma Sarah's REMEDIES

- ½ oz Sodium bicarbonate
- 1 oz Heavy Magnesium Carbonate
- 1 oz Calcium Carbonate
- 2 Drms Bismuth Oxycarbonate

Mix well together.

Dosage:

Teaspoonful in milk after meals.

I don't advise that you use any of these mixtures today as I'm quite sure there are excellent modern remedies that are probably much safer.

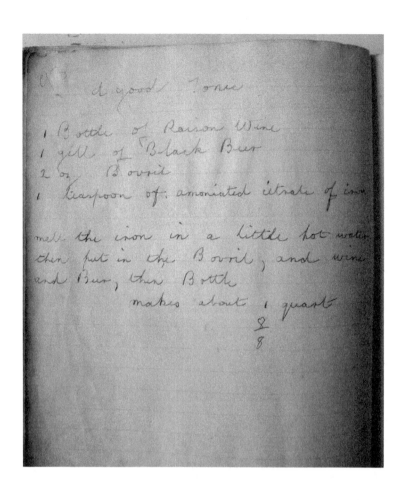

**Grandma Sarah's original homemade remedy
in her original handwriting**

Grandpa Norman

Grandpa Norman:
Quiet man and Unsung Hero

In 1914 Grandpa Norman left his job in the cotton mill and went to fight in the first World War (1914-1918), he was 21 years old. He enlisted in the Loyal North Lancashire Regiment where he rose to the rank of Sergeant. Research shows that later due lack of recruits and the senseless slaughter of millions of young men fighting in France, his battalion then amalgamated with the Kings Liverpool regiment, where he rose to the rank of 2nd Lieutenant commanding and fighting on the front line in France, and from what we learn from the history books, he must have seen and experienced first hand, the horrors and the inhumane suffering of the soldiers and everyone caught up in this awful part of our British History. The poet Wilfred Owen who was a British soldier and one of the leading poets of World War One, wrote in his poem Dulce et Decorum Est powerful descriptions from first-hand experience, about the shocking conditions faced by soldiers in the trenches and the effects of gas warfare. In the first line of the poem Wilfred Owen writes...

"Bent double like beggars under sacks, knock kneed, coughing like hags, we cursed through sludge" and in the next stanza writes,

"Gas ! Gas! Quick boys – An ecstasy of fumbling, fitting clumsy helmets just in time"

Wilfred Owen was killed in action a week before the war ended.

In Thomas Hardy's poem "The man he killed" written about the Boer War, is spoken from a soldiers point of view, asking himself that had he and the other soldier met under different circumstances, they probably would have bought each other a drink instead of trying to kill each other pointing out that ordinary men fight and kill not because they want to but because they are trained and forced to.

"Had he and I but met
By some old ancient inn,
We should have set us down to wet
Right many a nipperkin

Contrary to other poets of the time, who romanticised and glorified the war promising adventure, excitement and glory to persuade men sign up as soldiers, Wilfred Owen, Thomas Hardy.

And history shows, the reality of life on the front line turned out to be very different.

Grandpa Norman like many brave young men of World War One never spoke about his time in the war or the sights he'd witnessed, he returned home in 1918, to married life and to the lovely Grandma Sarah, and a year later, on the 6th of July 1919 their only son Ronald was born. Together they all settled down in a lovely house with a lovely garden in the Middle Hulton area on the outskirts of Bolton and they lived there for the rest of their lives. Grandpa Norman died in hospital in 1967 aged 74 yrs old and Grandma Sarah died in the same hospital in December 1970 aged 77 yrs old leaving behind precious and everlasting memories.

Grandpa Norman

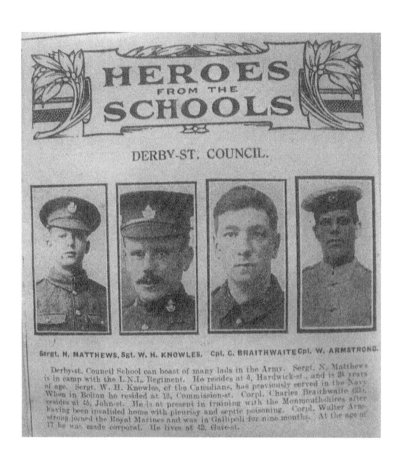

Grandpa Norman

Grandpa Norman

Grandpa Norman and his beloved Shed

Grandpa Norman was a typical grandpa, he spent lots of time with his grandchildren, a quiet, gentle, patient man, spent time in his beloved shed at the bottom of the garden, making items of furniture for the house.

He would also make small items of furniture for the neighbours and considering that his main occupation was a cotton mill worker, his natural skills with the plane and the lathe were amazing.

The smell of warm wood, glue and home-made wood stains coming from his shed was always a clue that he would be working on the latest footstool, cabinet or light fitting.

Here are a list of the home-made wood stains he made up and used.

Grandpa Norman

Light oak stain:

- Mix ¼ pint of liquid ammonia with ¾ of a pint of rainwater.
- Add Yellow Ochre to the shade required

Brown Oak Stain:

- 1oz of Permanganate of Potash
- Dissolve in 1 Pint of rainwater
- Add a little Brown or Burnt Umber

Try out on waste wood, if too light in colour add a little more Umber until the required colour is obtained.

Rosewood Stain:

- ½ lb of logwood ghips
- Boil in 1 quart of water
- A little soda will help to draw out the colour

3 French Polishes

3 French Polishes

- 1 Pint Metholated Spirits
- 5ozs Orange Shellac
- ¼ oz Gum Copal
- ¼ oz Gum Arabic

- 1 Pint Metholated Spirits
- 5ozs Orange Shellac
- 1 ½ Gum Sandarach

- 1 Pint Metholated Spirits
- 5ozs Orange Shellac
- ½ Gum Mastic

3 French Polishes

White Shellac can be substituted for Orange if a colourless polish is required.

Furniture Cream:

- ½ Pint of Turpintine.
- Scrape into it 2oz of White Wax.
- Leave this to dissolve all night.
- Melt ½ oz of Castile Soap in a pint of boiling water.
- Let this also stand all night.
- Mix these two together the next day, and Bottle it for further use.

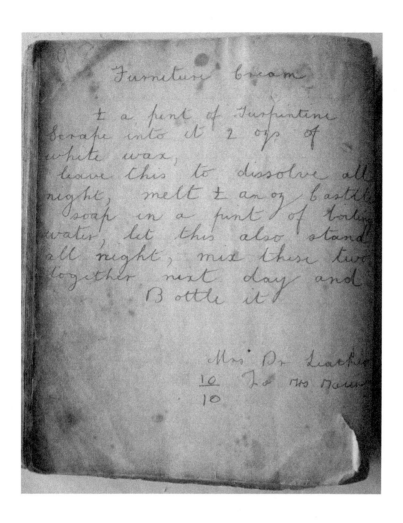

Grandpa Norman's original French polish tips in its original script

Grandpa Norman and Grandma Sarah

BOLTON

Bolton

Bolton Town Hall

Our Fab Town Hall

Saint Peter's Parish Church

A view of the Parish Church where I was married

Saturday, October 9th 1971 was my wedding day. At 3 O'clock I arrived at the church, with my dad, in the shiny black Rolls Royce Car all decked out with white satin ribbons and sprays of pretty flowers. It had been raining on and off all morning, but just as I arrived it had decided to brighten up and the sun shone.

The bells were ringing, the red carpet was laid, the choir had arrived, the Vicar was waiting and linking my arm was a very proud Dad.

We emerged an hour or so later, (my new Husband and I) with beaming smiles all around and on my finger was the remodelled wedding ring left to me by Grandma Sarah, no doubt she was looking down on us and smiling too.

St. Helens Road Methodist Church

This is the place where myself and all the family attended, we have so many happy memories of the people and friends who went there.

Our Children attended the Sunday School, the Youth Clubs, the Christmas parties, the plays, (I was in a couple) the trips out, the all night ping pong marathons in aid of orphaned children in Africa it was a very active place in the community.

Every Year at Christmas-time the church would hold a Christmas Fair. All manner of homemade goods could be bought, from scones with a cup of tea, to fancy goods and Christmas presents. Everyone who attended pulled together and donated or cooked or sewed, to help S.H.R. Methodist Church. It is still very active today, My husband's nanny was one of the first babies to be christened in the church in the 1890's. "Good Times".

St Peter's Parish Church

Inside Saint Peter's Parish Church

Deane Parish Church

Deane Parish Church in Bolton Lancashire, is a beautiful ancient Church which dates back to the year 1452. Many people from Grandma Sarah's family have been married at Deane Church including her only son Ronald in 1942.

It stands in a lovely, well-wooded area of Bolton.Many prominent people of Bolton are buried in the ancient peaceful churchyard, and some of Grandma's family members too.

Deane Parish Church is also mentioned in the Doomsday Book.

Deane Parish Church

Deane Parish Church in Bolton Lancashire

Many people from Grandma Sarah's family have been married at Deane Church including her only son Ronald in 1942.

Booth's Music Shop Bolton

This ancient little music shop is also on Churchgate, opposite Ye Olde Man and Scythe.

It has been one of Bolton's leading music shops since 1832 my own children used to buy their music books form Booths when they were learning to play the piano. It is the oldest music shop in the world and one of the oldest family businesses in the country. It's premises was originally the site of another famous inventor of Bolton who had a barber's shop there from 1760 - 1768 and in went on to invent the Water Frame.

Prestons of Bolton

Prestons of Bolton: The Diamond Centre of the World

Prestons of Bolton is known as the Diamond Centre of the North. The store was opened in 1869 by master Goldsmith and Diamond Merchant James Preston. The beautiful and aesthetic building stands on the corner of Deansgate and Bank Street in Bolton town centre.

It has become one of the most successful and famous jewellery stores in the country.

Ye Olde Man and Scythe in Bolton

Ye Olde Man and Scythe is in Churchgate in Bolton, it is opposite the famous Ye Olde Pastie Shoppe.

It is said to be haunted by the ghost of James Stanley the 7th Earl of Derby, who was reputed to have eaten his last meal there before he was taken outside and beheaded, for his part in the massacre of Bolton during the civil war, between the Royalists and the Parliamentarians. It is said his ghost has been seen sat in a chair in the corner of the pub where he sat before he was taken outside and executed.

The inscription written on top of the chair reads, 15th October 1651, In this chair James the 7th Earl of Derby sat at the Man and Scythe Inn, Churchgate Bolton immediately prior to his execution.

Ye Olde Pastie Shoppe Of Bolton

This Pastie shop is situated in Churchgate in the centre of Bolton. It was established in 1667 and is famous for it's handmade pasties. Staff are baking them from 5am each morning so that the freshly made pasties, pies and cakes are all ready for the customers when opening times comes.

The business has been in the same family since 1898 and it's still going strong today, although pasties are a northern dish, people come from all over the place to buy them. Hundreds of pasties are made every day and at Christmastime thousands are made and sold because they are so popular.

27 Wyndham Avenue Bolton

27 Wyndham Avenue Bolton

This is Grandma Sarah's house where I spent most of our courting days. We would visit her usually in the middle of the week and spend time sat on deck chairs at the back in her lovely cottage garden. It was always sunny then or at least it seemed so.

My husband (boyfriend then), would cut her grass for her and mend anything that was broken in and around the house.

In return we would feast on homemade scones, potato cakes , homemade bread and lemon curd, and copious cups of tea.

The Octagon Theatre

BOLTON'S Famous People

Bolton's
Famous People

Kenneth Wolstenholme

Kenneth Wolstenholme was born in Worsley not far from Bolton, he went to Farnworth Grammar School, (quite near to the school where I work).

He started career as a journalist with a Manchester newspaper.

In World War two, he was a qualified pilot, and he flew many brave sorties over occupied Europe for his bravery he was awarded the DFC and Bar. After the war he became a freelance journalist working for the BBC then he moved to television.

He is best remembered for his commentary of the 1966 World Cup Final at Wembley Stadium when in injury time a small number of the crowd invaded the pitch and Kenneth Wolstenholme said: "They think it's all over," but then Geoff Hurst scored another goal which prompted him to say, "IT IS NOW!"

Samuel Crompton

The Spinning Mule-1779
Samuel Crompton 1753-1827

So be proud of this your township,
he helped put on the map.
This child whose name
was Samuel,
who became a gradely chap.

Sheila Stephens Orrell, Bolton

Bolton like many towns in the North of England has produced their fair share of famous people.

This is a picture of Samuel Crompton's grave, he is buried in the grounds of Bolton Parish Church.

Samuel Crompton invented the Spinning Mule in 1799. This machine helped the cotton industry take a massive leap forward, and the cotton industry in Bolton grew at a tremendous rate and came to dominate the town. There is a statue of Samuel Crompton situated in Nelson Square in Bolton town centre.

Fred Dibnah MBE

Steeplejack, Television Presenter and Mechanical Engineer

Fredrick Dibnah was born on the 28th April 1938 in Bolton.

He began his working life as a joiner before he became a steeplejack.

After completing his two years National Service in the armed forces, Fred was demobbed in 1962 and returned to steeplejacking but the decline in the cotton industry affected his work. Mills all over the town were closing and he struggled to get work.

Then he was asked to repair the Bolton Parish Church, and the publicity that followed helped to boost his flagging business ensuring that he was always in employment.

He also made repairs to Bolton's stunning Town Hall where decades of wear had caused serious damage to the clock tower.

Decades of wear had caused serious damage to the clock tower. Fred repaired the clock tower and gilded the golden sphere at the top of the building. Whilst he was working on the town hall he was approached by the BBC Look North West News programme, who wanted to interview him, the interview took place at the top of the town hall with Fred perched outside on his scaffolding.

This led to television appearances and further interviews, most of them hundreds of feet in the air, and he was contacted by a producer with a view to making a documentary and this was a great success, he was asked to do many more over the years and in 1979 Fred won the BAFTA award for best documentary.

Fred Dibnah was recognised as the stereotypical northern working man and he was held in high esteem by many British people, he was unique and his like we will never see again, he was one of a kind.

Fred Dibnah died Bolton Hospice on the 6th of November 2004 he was 66 years old, he is buried in Tonge Cemetery on the outskirts of Bolton town centre, thousands turned out to watch his funeral. His coffin was towed through the centre of Bolton by his restored tractor engine which was driven by his son and a possession of steam-powered vehicles made their way to Bolton Parish Church.

Today a bronze statue of stands in Bolton town centre in memory of Fred Dibnah MBE.

A play titled "The Demolition Man" was staged at Bolton's Octagon Theatre in tribute to Fred's early life.

James Stanley

**The Spot, marked by a cross where James Stanley Lord
Derby was beheaded**

The End

CPSIA information can be obtained
at www.ICGtesting.com
Printed in the USA
LVOW06s2057050917
547614LV00009B/65/P